A GUIDE TO CHRISTIAN ETHICS

A Guide to Christian Ethics

MORRIS A. INCH

RESOURCE *Publications* • Eugene, Oregon

A GUIDE TO CHRISTIAN ETHICS

Copyright © 2013 Morris A. Inch. All rights reserved. Except for brief quotations in critical publications or reviews, no part of this book may be reproduced in any manner without prior written permission from the publisher. Write: Permissions, Wipf and Stock Publishers, 199 W. 8th Ave., Suite 3, Eugene, OR 97401.

Resource Publications
An Imprint of Wipf and Stock Publishers
199 W. 8th Ave., Suite 3
Eugene, OR 97401

www.wipfandstock.com

ISBN 13: 978-1-62564-038-3

Manufactured in the U.S.A.

Contents

Preface | vii

Acknowledgment | ix

I Prime Texts
1. The Greatest Commandment | 3
2. The Decalogue | 10
3. The Golden Rule | 17
4. In Christ | 25

II Divine Mandates
5. Church Mandate | 37
6. Family Mandate | 45
7. Labor Mandate | 53
8. Government Mandate | 60

III Cardinal Virtues
9. Justice | 69
10. Prudence | 78
11. Temperance | 85
12. Fortitude | 92

IV Theological Virtues
- **13** Faith | 101
- **14** Hope | 108
- **15** Love | 116

V Miscellaneous
- **16** Sage Sayings | 125

    Bibliography | 133

Preface

GUIDE TO CHRISTIAN ETHICS speaks for itself. This is with the intent of setting forth a vibrant Christian morality, repudiating legalism on the one hand and cultural compromise on the other. As for the former, Jesus exclaimed: "Woe to you, teachers of the law and Pharisees, you hypocrites! You give a tenth of your spices—mint, dill and cumin. But you have neglected the more important matters of the law—justice, mercy and faith" (Matt. 23:23). *Legalism* thus attempts to reduce ethics to a meticulous code of behavior, without consideration for the constructive purposes it is supposed to serve.

As for the latter, "They dwell in their own countries, but simply as sojourners. As citizens, they share in all things with others, and yet endure all things as if foreigners. Every foreign land is to them as their native country, and every land of their birth as a land of strangers."[1] Consequently, they should serve a dynamic catalyst, rather than simply embrace cultural norms.

Initially, the text explores several pertinent Scriptural references. This serves to focus on divine revelation as normative for Christian ethics. In this regard, "Do not conform any longer to the patterns of this world, but be transformed by the renewing of your mind. Then you will be able to test and approve what will is—his good, pleasing, and perfect will" (Rom. 12:2).

The discussion then turns to a consideration of divine mandates. In particular, those concerning the church, family, labor,

1. *Epistle of Diognetus*, V.

Preface

and government. These accent social ethics from a Christian perspective.

The notion of virtue next invites our attention. First, in connection with the cardinal virtues—thought to provide the foundation of an ethical system. In particular, as concerns justice, prudence, temperance, and fortitude.

Second, regarding the theological virtues—associated with God's redemptive activity. Expressly, with faith, hope, and love. Accordingly, Paul writes: "And now remains faith, hope and love. But the greatest of these is love" (1 Cor. 12:13).

It remains to touch on select sage sayings. These played an important role in the village culture in which I was raised. Moreover, they continue to lend support to moral resolve over the years.

Notwithstanding, considerable ambiguity surrounds moral behavior. "But isn't this a recipe for moral chaos?" Edward Tivnan rhetorically inquires. "Surely, some things are simply right or wrong. They are indeed. But I will argue that the only way we can create a decent society is to understand why we disagree so strongly and learn to live with our disagreements, all the while fighting for our convictions (but never forgetting that we might actually be wrong)."[2]

Some things are simply right or wrong. I find no way to justify the terrorist who indiscriminately takes the lives of the general populace. Let alone sacrificing impressionable youth to serve his purpose. Then to portray the activity as a matter of religious devotion.

Conversely, some matters are more complicated. As with the notion of a *just war*. Is such admissible? If so, under what conditions? Certainly not as an excuse to disregard human life or for wanton destruction.

So the stage is set for the discussion to follow. May it contribute to an imposing task that continues to solicit our collective endeavor. I have also drawn on my previous publications in unprecedented fashion. Qualifications aside, it thus constitutes virtually a lifetime of ethical reflection.

---

2. Tivnan, *The Moral Imagination*, 7.

Acknowledgment

As on previous occasions, I am deeply appreciative of my beloved wife Joan, for her crucial contribution in reading, correcting and original formatting of the text. Also, a hearty thank you to Diane Higdon for her help in learning and maneuvering through a new word processing program.

I

Prime Texts

1

The Greatest Commandment

SEVERAL BRIEF TEXTUAL STUDIES initiate our consideration of Christian ethics. This is in keeping with the conviction that Scripture serves as the norm for Christian faith and practice. In this regard, "All Scripture is God breathed and is useful for teaching, rebuking, correcting and training in righteousness" (2 Tim. 3:16).

Teacher," a certain scribe inquired of Jesus, "which is the greatest commandment in the Law?" (Matt. 22:36). It appears to have been a stock question, meant to ascertain whether Jesus adhered to the religious tradition. This concern carried over into other related issues, as documented at considerable length in the biblical text.

"'Love the Lord your God with all your heart and with all your soul and with all your mind,'" Jesus replied. This was originally cited in association with the *Shema*, embraced as the cornerstone of Jewish faith: "Hear, O Israel: The Lord our God the Lord is one" (Deut. 6:4). "This is the first and greatest commandment," Jesus then confirmed his intent (Matt. 22:38).

"And the second is like it," he continued: "'Love your neighbor as yourself' (cf. Lev. 19:18). All the Law and the Prophets hang on these two commandments." While two commandments, they are inseparable.

"In an age when the word 'love' is greatly abused, it is important to remember that the primary component of biblical love is not affection but commitment. Warm feelings of gratitude may fill our consciousness as we consider all that God has done for us, but is not warm feelings that Deut. 6:5 demands of us but rather stubborn, unwavering commitment."[1] The same could be said of the love we extend to our neighbor.

Such qualifies as *hard love*. Or as C. S. Lewis observes, "Because God loves us, he tries to make us lovable." Only then can we realize something of our potential for living in God's world, by means of his grace. Whereupon, it serves as an incentive to strive for excellence.

Now our professed devotion to God does not substitute for our unavailability to one another, nor the reverse. "Away with the noise of your songs!" the oracle declares. "I will not listen to the music of your harps. But let justice roll on like a river, righteousness like a never-failing stream!" (Amos 5:23–24).

"We love because he first loved us," John reminds his readers. "If anyone says, 'I love God,' yet hates his brother, he is a liar. For anyone who does not love his brother, whom he has seen, cannot love God, whom he has not seen. And he has given us this command: Whoever loves God must also love his brother" (1 John 4:19–21). We are thus incited to love as an expression of gratitude.

While a person may insist that he or she loves God, this is impossible to demonstrate. "Even if he goes through the outward motions of devotion to God, prayer, attendance at worship, and so on, it may still be all empty show. But a person cannot so easily deceive others regarding his love for his fellow Christians; since they can be seen, the person's relation with them is also visible."[2] Admittedly, there is still the possibility of deception even in this instance.

In addition, we are alerted to the *fervency* required of the response. "I know your deeds, your hard work and your perseverance. I know that you cannot tolerate wicked men, that you have tested those who claim to be apostles but are not, and have found

---

1. Hare, *Matthew*, 260.
2. Marshall, *The Epistles of John*, 225–26.

The Greatest Commandment

them false. You have persevered and have endured hardships for my name, and have not grown weary," the oracle assures the Ephesian congregation. "Yet I hold this against you: You have forsaken your first love" (Rev. 2:2-4).

"Remember the height from which you have fallen! Repent and do the things you did at first." If not, do not expect clemency.

I recall a classmate from college. He was an especially devout person, actively engaged in devotional practices and Christian outreach. However, he had not ascertained how God would have him invest his life. Whatever the means, I anticipated that he would pursue his calling with exceptional zeal.

It came as a surprise that he matriculated to the same seminary I had chosen. While not sensing that God had called him to the pastoral ministry, he thought a year of theological studies would be profitable. He did not return for a second year.

Time passed before I again encountered him. He enthusiastically alerted me to the fact that he had found his calling. It consisted of teaching in West Africa. Consequently, he felt admirably fulfilled.

Again time passed when I received notice that he had passed away. It seems that he had contracted a tropical disease, for which his body had no immunity. He was buried abroad, among those he had fervently served.

Still later on, I was engaged in a short-term teaching assignment in Nigeria. Scanning the vista, I could make out a single white cross half way between the chapel and village. Upon investigation, it turned out not to be that of my former classmate, but another missionary who had perished on the field. It, nonetheless, brought back many cherished memories of a stalwart disciple and cherished friend.

A loving response also implies *obedience*. "Does the Lord delight in burnt offerings and sacrifices as much as in obeying the voice of the Lord?" Samuel rhetorically inquired. "To obey is better than sacrifice, and to heed is better than the fat of rams" (1 Sam. 15:22).

Herein lies the critical difference between serving the Living God and lifeless idols. As for the former, one must weigh carefully divine instruction, and pursue righteousness. As for the latter, a token gift may suffice. Obedience thus appears as a deterrent of idolatry.

Incidentally, idolatry can take many forms. I have an idol sitting inconspicuously on one of my bookshelves. It dates to the time of the Jewish Monarchy. It is a replica of a bull—meant to represent Baal, and likely a household artifact.

Idolatry reveals various levels of sophistication, even in antiquity. It appears for some that the deity is actually present, while for others it is simply representative. In any case, the Baal idol was taken seriously—primarily as a means of securing fertility: concerning one's offspring, herds, and harvests.

According to the initial humanist manifesto, "Though we consider the religious forms and ideas of our fathers no longer adequate, the quest for the good life is still the central task for mankind. Man is at last becoming aware that he alone is responsible for the realization of the world of his dreams, that he has within himself the power for its achievement."[3] Idolatry is as idolatry does. Hence, when human ideals replace divine directives as matters of ultimate concern, we serve idols of our own making. Consequently, it bears repeating: "To obey is better than sacrifice."

Another inescapable feature of the prime commandment is *service*. "No one can serve two masters," Jesus declared. "Either he will hate the one and love the other, or he will be devoted to the one and despise the other. You cannot serve both God and Money" (Matt. 6:24). *Money* is not the culprit, but the *love of money*. "Some people, eager for money, have wandered from the faith and pierced themselves with many griefs"(1 Tim. 6:10).

Acquisition plays a legitimate role in a biblical ethic. In this regard, the rabbis promoted the dual virtues of industry and generosity. Concerning the former, it was said that a person cannot properly observe the Sabbath unless he or she had been industrious throughout the week.

Concerning the latter, Jesus watched the people putting their offerings into the temple treasury. Many affluent individuals contributed large sums. "But a poor widow came and put in two

---

3. *Humanist Manifesto I*, fifteen.

The Greatest Commandment

very small copper coins, worth only a fraction of a penny" (Mark 12:42). Summoning his disciples, Jesus observed: "I tell you the truth, this poor widow has put more into the treasury than all the others. They all gave out of their wealth; but she, out of her poverty, put in everything—all she had to live on." Consequently, it would appear that genuine generosity cannot be measured by how much one gives, but by how much remains.

Moreover, we are reminded that serving God anticipates considering the needs of others along with our own. Jesus illustrated this feature by washing his disciples' feet. "Do you understand what I have done for you?" he then inquired. "You call me 'Teacher' and 'Lord'. And rightly so, for that is what I am. Now that I, your Lord and Teacher, have washed your feet, you also should wash one another's feet" (John 12-14). Thus we would conclude that service is also a privilege.

Worthy of note, we are also enjoined to love our neighbor as ourselves. By depreciating self, we cultivate a negative form of pride. Which is to say, we give undue attention to self, rather than dealing with other pressing concerns.

Then, too, since life is derived from God, to despise the gift is to dishonor its giver. Life is inherently good, providing that we live it according to divine guidelines Other-wise, it readily unravels.

I have heard it said that those who love God can do as they please; because if they actually love God, they will do as he pleases. So it would seem in keeping with the above line of reasoning. Observe these coupled commandments, and life comes into focus. Avoid them at high risk.

With such in mind, we turn our attention to select commentary by the early church fathers—by way of further exploring this current theme. Polycarp reminds the Philippian congregation of Paul's correspondence in which they find the means of maturing in the Christian faith, "which, being followed by hope, and preceded by love towards God, and Christ, and our neighbor, 'is the mother of us all' (cf. Gal. 4:26). For if anyone be inwardly possessed of these graces he has fulfilled the command of righteousness, since he that has love is far from all sin."[4]

"His love is not confined to any national group or spiritual elite. It is a love that proceeds from the fact that he is love. He loves people because he is the kind of God he is."[5] It is uniquely and grandly demonstrated in the gift of his *one and only Son* (cf. John 3:16).

A commensurate love is thus solicited. One that springs from a genuine gratitude, as previously noted in passing. One that extends to Christ for his vicarious sacrifice, and readily complies with divine instruction. Such distances a person *from all sin*, since there is no compatibility between the two.

Jesus was put to death by those who took issue with him, and who continue to persecute his followers, Justin Martyr allows, "while all of us pray for you, and for all men, as our Christ and Lord taught us to do, when He enjoined us to pray even for our enemies, and to love them that hate us, and to bless them who curse us."[6] This is in keeping with Paul's admonition: "be joyful always, pray continually, give thanks in all circumstance, for this is God's will for you in Christ Jesus" (1 Thess. 5:15-17).

Pray without ceasing, since it said that more is accomplished by prayer than this world realizes. Love even when hated and afflicted, for love triumphs over adversity. Bless even when cursed. In these and other regards, join with the early believers alluded to in Justin Martyr's tractate.

"The perfect man ought therefore to practice love, and thence to haste to the divine friendship, fulfilling the commandments from love," Clement of Alexandria enjoins. "And loving one's enemies does not mean loving wickedness, or impiety, or adultery, or theft; but the thief, the impious, the adulterer, not as far as he sins, and in respect of the actions by which he stains the name of man, but as he is a man, and the work of God"[7] Accordingly,

---

4. *The Epistle of Polycarp to the Philippians,* III.
5. Clement of Alexandria, *The Stromata,* IV. xiv.
6. Justin Martyr, *Dialogue with Trypho,* CXXXIII.
7. Clement of Alexandria, *The Stromata,* IV, xiv.

distinguish between substance and activity, between man and his perverse ways.

From a compatible perspective, love a person not simply for what he is but might become as a means of God's grace. See in him the potential for which he was intended. Do not settle for less than spiritual maturity, whether with regard to self or others.

"Now fear works abstinence from what is evil; but love exhorts to the doing of good, by building up to the point of spontaneousness; that one may hear from the Lord, 'I call you no longer servants, but friends,' and may now with confidence apply himself to prayer." Although *fear* may be a legitimate deterrent, it falls short of building a feasible alternative.

Consequently, it remains for *love* to cultivate the doing of good. In that "perfect love drives out fear, because fear has to do with punishment" (1 John 4:18). As a result, one can confidently apply him or herself to prayer. This fosters a spontaneity expressive of one's spiritual orientation. It is not something labored, let alone pretentious. Clement subsequently concludes, "We are therefore to love Jesus equally with God. And he loves Christ Jesus who does His will and keeps His commandments"[8] Since the love of God and Christ draw from the same impetus.

Those who Jesus bid come, he also sent forth to proclaim the good news. In this regard, the risen Christ informed his disciples: "But you will receive power when the Holy Spirit comes on you, and you will be my witnesses in Jerusalem, and in all Judea and Samaria, and to the ends of the earth" (Acts 1:8).

Meanwhile, they had been carefully instructed by Jesus as to how they should behave. This involved both word and deed. Thus from early on they were designated as Christians (cf. Acts 11:26), which is to say followers of Christ—thus emulating his teaching. So it is that the quest for a vibrant Christian ethic continues unabated and provocatively inviting.

---

8. Ibid., VII, xii.

2

The Decalogue

"Do not think that I have come to abolish the Law or the Prophets," Jesus cautioned; "I have not come to abolish them but to fulfill them" (Matt. 5:17). With such in mind, we turn our attention to the *decalogue*—concerning the ten commandments. Its importance can hardly be overstated. The rabbis "speculated that it was prepared on the eve of creation in anticipation of subsequent use; they asserted that as each commandment was sounded from the lofty height of Sinai it filled the world with a pleasing aroma; they concluded that all nature hushed to hear every word as it was spoken."[1] It was preserved from one generation to the next as a cherished legacy.

It would appear that the decalogue consisted of core teaching, which would be elaborated subsequently in its covenant setting. The latter was fashioned after a vassal treaty, wherein God pledged to intercede on behalf of his people on condition of their loyalty. It consisted of five segments: preamble, historical prologue, stipulations, sanctions, and provision for renewal. As succinctly expressed, the *pre-amble* declared: "Moses proclaimed to the Israelites all that the Lord had com-manded him concerning them" (Deut. 1:3). As such, it identifies Yahweh as the heavenly sovereign, on whose behalf Moses extended the treaty for ratification.

---

1. Inch, *Scripture As Story*, 35.

The Decalogue

Conversely, the *historical prologue* recalled God's lavish provision for his chosen people in the past. Examples were readily available: "Yahweh had delivered his people from bondage in Egypt, graciously met with them at Sinai, sustained them in the wilderness, and given them recent victories in the Trans-Jordan. This he had done in spite of their persisting waywardness."[2]

The major portion of the covenant consisted of *stipulations*. Having taken great care to structure life according to divine precepts, it concludes with the injunction: "The Lord your God commands you this day to follow these decrees and laws; carefully observe them with all your heart and all your soul" (Deut. 26:16). There follows a promissory note: "He has declared he will set you in praise, fame and honor high above all the nations he has made and that you will be a people holy to the Lord your God, as he promised."

The *sanctions* contrast the fortunes of the righteous and wicked. If obedient, the people could expect to be blessed *in the city and in the country*, by way of their posterity, *the crops of your land*, and *the young of your flocks*. So also with *your basket*, and *your kneading trough, when you come in and go out*. In every way that genuinely matters. If disobedient, they will be cursed in all the ways cited above.

The final section deals with *covenant renewal*. Such would allow the people to renew their commitment in the light of changing circumstances. As when they ceased to be a nomadic people, and settled in the land. Consequently, it would preserve essential continuity in the context of legitimate accommodation.

Thus alerted to the character of the covenant, we return to the decalogue as its central focus. Worthy of note, the first four commandments deal with one's relationship to the Almighty, while the remainder pertains to inter-personal relationships. Thus the dual commandment of loving God without exception and our neighbor as ourselves is greatly augmented.

"I am the Lord your God, who brought you out of Egypt, out of the land of slavery," Yahweh declares. "You shall have no other gods before me" (Exod. 20:2–3). This is meant to disallow other deities.

2. Ibid., 41.

In greater detail this "first 'word' takes aim at atheism (we must have a God), idolatry (we must have Yahweh as our God), polytheism (we must have the Lord God alone), and formalism (we must live, fear and serve the Lord with our heart, soul, and strength, and mind). The ground of all morality begins here."[3] Apart from this grounding of morality in the gracious will of a benevolent deity, it is given to partisan agendas and tempting compromise.

"You shall not make for yourself an idol in the form of anything in heaven above or on the earth beneath or in the waters below," the text continues. "You shall not bow down to them or worship them; for I, the Lord your God, am a jealous God, punishing the children for the sin of the fathers to the third and fourth generation of those who hate me, but showing love in a thousand generations of those who love me and keep my commandments." The prohibition extends to fashioning idols or worshiping them, since both contribute to the practice of idolatry.

It would seemingly include images of the Almighty for at least three reasons: "First, they would be inadequate expressions of the divine reality. Second, they would impose human misunderstanding. Third, they might give the impression that God could be localized in some manner or other."[4] Initially, *they would be inadequate* to express the divine reality. Accordingly, they would fail to manifest his glory.

Along with this concern, they impose alien features. Such as are derived not only from human finiteness, but our fallen condition. So that our perception is distorted; and in the process, intensified. In this regard, God declares: "As the heavens are higher than the earth, so are my ways higher than your ways and my thoughts than your thoughts" (Isa. 55:9).

Finally, they could *give the impression God might be localized*, as with pagan deities, which represent their respective constituencies. Conversely, the psalmist observes: "The Lord has established his throne in heaven and his kingdom rules over all" (103:19).

---

3. Kaiser, Jr., *Toward Old Testament Ethics*, 85.
4. Inch, *op. cit.*, 16.

The Decalogue

The accompanying rationale recognizes the social implications of our behavior. What one does or fails to do inevitably impacts on others. Even so, the Lord pledges to lessen the effect of wicked behavior, while intensifying that of righteous resolve. This led to the observation that if God were to throw dice, they would be loaded.

"You shall not misuse the name of the Lord your God, for the Lord will not hold anyone guiltless who misuses his name." The rabbis extended this prohibition to a wide range of unacceptable practices. Not surprising, it disallowed profanity. Since this involves contempt or irreverence of that which is sacred.

Furthermore, God's name was not to be used in a trivial fashion. That is to say, without due consideration. Such as is commonly done by way of emphasis.

Neither was his name to be used in jest. While humor was cultivated, it was not to be at the expense of the sacred. Accordingly, the sage observes: "There is a time for everything, and a season for every activity under heaven: a time to weep and a time to laugh" (Eccles. 3:1, 4).

Nor was his name to be spoken thoughtlessly. As if reciting the name had some merit in and of itself. As when going through the motions were a substitute for heartfelt intercession. Whether in these or other ways, God is demeaned, and persons suffer from their impiety.

Remember the Sabbath day by keeping it holy. Six days you shall labor and do all your work, but the seventh day is a Sabbath to the Lord your God. On it you shall not do any work, neither you, nor your son or daughter, nor your manservant, nor your animals, nor the alien within your gates." "And just as it is impossible to describe the beauty of a sunset to one who has never seen it, so one cannot fully convey the import and majesty that the Sabbat has for the observant Jew. Intellect will not suffice in unlocking its mysteries and hidden spiritual treasures, nor can it fully grasp the significance of that day."[5] So that its profound significance cannot be adequately articulated, but needs to be appreciatively experienced.

---

5. Eckstein, *How Firm a Foundation*, 62

Sabbath observance is couched in the context of extended labor. Work serves as a means of self-fulfillment and responsible contribution to human welfare. "Go to the ant, you sluggard," the sage enjoins; "consider its ways and be wise!" (Prov. 6:6). I anticipated this injunction as a child, and was impressed not only by the industry of the ants, but the disposition to coordinate their activity.

In Jewish tradition, one counts toward the Sabbath. Sunday thus being the first day, and so on. Anticipation is calculated to build as the week progresses. Moreover, persons are encouraged to engage life in Sabbath perspective.

Sabbath regulations are of two sorts: negative and positive. As for the former, the notion of *rest* alerts one of a change of venue. While there will be continued activity, it will be of a different sort. For instance, observant Jews will refrain from activity thought analogous to divine creation. Accordingly, food is prepared in advance, in anticipation of subsequently partaking of it. Other more common practices are thought especially suitable for the Sabbath. As an example, an orthodox rabbi concluded: "Sex is most enjoyable in a Sabbath context.

Conversely, the positive regulations are meant to fine-tune the Sabbath experience. Such as the reading of Torah and prayer, in the home and at the Synagogue. Thereby to enhance piety. This serves to put life in perspective, along the lines of a *sacred canopy*. Then, by way of contrast, to the *jungle code*—as graphically expressed by my maternal grandmother: "Everyone for himself, and the Devil gets the hindmost."

Incidentally, the Christian's appropriation of Sabbath observance has long been a subject of controversy. Conversely, Jewish tradition seems not to have thought it binding on others. Some, however, held that it could be embraced on a voluntary basis.

The focus now shifts to interpersonal relationships. "Honor your father and your mother, so that you may live long in the land the Lord your God is giving you." This is recalled as "the first commandment with promise" (Eph. 6:2). As such, it is set forth as instrumental in a healthy society.

The Decalogue

Honor of parents implies respect, obedience, and love. *Respect* first of all, since they are our natural mentors. This brings to mind the humorous comment of a Jewish fellow whose mother informed him: "When I want your opinion, I will tell you what it is."

Respect also because they are our providers. We are indebted to them for life itself, and their subsequent investment. It is a debt that we cannot adequately pay without showing deference to them.

Obedience is coupled with respect. Not in a begrudging manner but heartily. Not in token fashion but as common practice. Viewed from covenant perspective, where God is honored and the people blessed.

Love rounds out the triad. This includes taking care of their parents' physical, social, and spiritual needs. Earlier on, as the opportunity afforded itself; and pro-gressively as they age. It was also thought to extend beyond life as a treasured memory of the past. Such as might be recalled by proper memorials.

"You shall not murder." This is meant to preserve the sanctity of life. While not excluding the possibility of capital punishment, it would seem to restrain the practice. Not only are persons to refrain from wanton killing, but are charged with protecting the lives of others.

The prohibition extends to our inner disposition. "You have heard that it was said to the people long ago, 'Do not murder, and anyone who murders will be subject to judgment,'" Jesus allowed. "But I tell you that anyone who is angry with his brother will be subject to judgment" (Matt. 5:21–22).

"You shall not commit adultery." While marital fidelity is the primary focus, the rabbis extended this prohibition to embrace other forms of unacceptable sexual behavior. As an example, "No one is to approach any close relative to have sexual relations" (Lev. 18:6). As another, "Do not lie with a man as one lies with a woman" (18:22). In conclusion, "Keep my requirement and do not follow any of the detestable customs that were practiced before you came and do not defile yourselves with them. I am the Lord your God" (18:30).

"Live by the Spirit," Paul urges his readers, "and you will not gratify the desires of the sinful nature" (Gal. 5:16). Consequently, the rabbis urged their constituency to build fences lest they succumb to evil inclinations. This led a certain rabbi to conclude that there is nothing wrong in building fences as long as we do not worship them.

"You shall not steal." "According to rabbinic tradition, one is guilty whether he or she brazenly robs in public or in secret; whether in taking possession from another or kidnaping the person; whether involving much or little, whether outright or with usury; whether concerning property or reputation."[6]

In a peasant society, theft could endanger life itself. In a covenant society, it was both an affront to God, and a violation of community. It could not be tolerated even in more subtle connections, such as demeaning one's reputation.

"You shall not give false testimony against your neighbor." The seriousness of the injunction can be seen in that it could result in a death sentence. Even were that not the case, it constitutes an act of injustice.

Initially, one is encouraged to dwell on what is true (cf. Phil. 4:8). Moreover, one is to articulate truth. Then, finally, one should embody truth. That is to say, not only talk the talk, but walk the walk.

"You shall not covet your neighbor's house. You shall not covet your neighbor's wife, or his manservant or maidservant, his ox or his donkey, or anything that belongs to your neighbor." "*House* means 'household', in the early sense of the word, and the thought of 'wife' is primary. *Ox* and *ass* are the typical wealth of the bronze age peasant or semi-nomad, for whom the perplexities of developed society have not yet arisen."[7]

"This final interdict makes explicit what has been implicit up to this point: that our predatory desires are the root to our perverse practices. In this connection, we are reminded that man is his own worst enemy."[8]

---

6. Inch, *op. cit.*, 37.
7. Cole, *Exodus*, 161.
8. Inch, *op. cit.*, 38.

3

The Golden Rule

"So in everything, do to others what you would have them do to you," Jesus admonished (Matt. 7:12). This has come to be designated as *The Golden Rule*. In its negative form, it appears in a variety of sources. For instance, we read in the apocryphal book of Tobit "And what you hate, do not do to any one" (4:15). Conversely, it only appears on this occasion in its positive counterpart.

"Some writers hold that the shift from negative to positive is without any particular significance. However, in its negative form the Golden Rule could be satisfied by doing nothing. The positive form moves us to action on behalf of others; it calls us to do for others all those things that we would appreciate being done for us."[1] As such, it seizes the moral initiative.

It serves to get a running start. Matthew's Gospel has a didactic purpose. One of its distinctive features "is that the teaching of Jesus is collected into five sections. The Sermon on the Mount (chaps. 5–7) is the first of these blocks. The others are Instructions to the Twelve (chap. 10), Parables of the Kingdom (chap. 13), Life in the Christian Community (chap. 18), and Eschatological

---

1. Mounce, *Matthew*, 66.

17

Judgment (chaps. 23–25)."[2] Each block concludes with a formula approximating: "When Jesus had finished saying these things."

Most conclude that the Sermon on the Mount constitutes a collection of Jesus's sayings, rather than a single discourse. This would account for excerpts appearing elsewhere in Luke's Gospel, although we would assume that Jesus repeated himself on occasion. Even if a collection, it might be compiled from a limited span of time, whether several days or simply early on in Jesus' public ministry.

We are alerted to the fact that Jesus taught his disciples in the presence of the multitude. Not long before the two groups were indistinguishable, but that was no longer the case. As for the former, they had decided to follow Jesus. As would students who matriculate for a course of study.

This recalls a former colleague who would greet his students with the observation, "Life has become much simpler now that you have signed on as students. Since you are students, you *will* study; since you are students, you *will* eat properly; since you are students, you *will* get proper rest; since you are students, you *will* exercise." Needless to say, the life of the disciple was no less focused.

As for the latter, the multitude was not monolithic. Some were genuinely searching, while others simply curious. In any case, the two groups had taken leave of one another. While perhaps obscure at the moment, their departure would become more pronounced with the passing of time and with prospect for eternity.

As for Jesus, he was a model instructor. If for no other reason, he lived what he taught. This singled him out from the rest, who could only admonish his or her students to excel beyond themselves. Then, too, Jesus made good use of the teaching resources available to him. In particular, his masterful employment of parables comes to mind.

The Sermon on the Mount begins with a series of beatitudes. Initially, "Blessed are the poor in spirit, for theirs is the kingdom of heaven" (Matt. 5:2). That is, blessed are those who realize how

---

2. Ibid., 36

desperate their condition and turn to God in their plight. As over against some who think they can fend for themselves.

"Blessed are those who mourn, for they will be comforted." Such as are filled with deep regret for their waywardness, and troubled by the pervasive evidence of evil in the world. In due time, they will be comforted, and even now God consoles them.

"Blessed are the meek, for they will inherit the earth." "Jesus carried out his messianic ministry, not as a Zealot intent on establishing by force a political kingdom, but as one who lived a life of humble and sacrificial service to God and his fellow human beings. This is the meekness to which Jesus calls his followers."[3] Conversely, the aggressive will be unable to enjoy their ill-gotten gains.

"Blessed are those who hunger and thirst after righteousness, for they will be filled." "As the deer pants for streams of water, so my soul pants for you, O God," the psalmist allows (42:1). This encouraged him to inquire, "When can I go and meet with God?" The sooner, the better. Preferably for an extended time, along with predictable blessing.

"Blessed are the merciful, for they will be shown mercy." *Mercy* is a compre-hensive term, including compassion and forgiveness. As for the former, a Canaanite woman pled with Jesus: "Lord, Son of David, have mercy on me! My daughter is suffering terribly from demon-possession" (Matt. 15:22). Whereupon, Jesus granted her petition. As for the latter, Jesus admonished: "Forgive, and it will be forgiven" (Luke 6:37). Mercy is exemplified in both instances.

"Blessed are the pure in heart, for they will see God." "Do not be deceived," Paul enjoins: "God cannot be mocked. A man reaps what he sows. The one who sows to please his sinful nature, from that nature will reap destruction; the one who sows to please the Spirit, from the Spirit will reap eternal life" (Gal. 6:7–8). Consequently, let us not grow weary in well doing, but press on with singular devotion.

"Blessed are the peacemakers, for they will be called sons of God." The peace that Jesus advocates is not passive compliance,

3. Ibid., 39

but persisting initiatives. It requires that we learn from past experience, while recognizing the uniqueness of subsequent events. As *sons of God*, persons emulate his disposition.

Finally, "Blessed are those who are persecuted because of righteousness, for theirs is the kingdom of God." Those who actively pursue their calling, "and consequently are impelled to take a stand on moral issues and to support controversial or unpopular causes must expect to be ridiculed and maligned. Such hostility is unpleasant but not crushing to those who are convinced that Gods' approbation is more important by far than fleeting popularity."[4]

Jesus' extended discourse elaborates the theme in greater detail. We will touch on the intervening text briefly before considering *The Golden Rule* more explicitly. "In the same way (as a lamp is set on a stand), let your light shine before men, that they may see your good deeds and praise your Father in heaven" (5:16). Not as a means of aggrandizing self, but honoring the Almighty.

Having affirmed his accord with the Law and the Prophets, Jesus cautions: "Anyone who breaks one of the least of these commandments and teaches others to do the same will be called least in the kingdom of heaven, but whoever practices and teaches these commands will be called great in the kingdom of heaven" (5:19). Accordingly, the rabbis reasoned that those who were meticulous with lesser matters would be disposed to observing more substantial concerns. Jesus, however, confirms that this is not necessarily the case.

He next introduces the formula: "You have heard that it was said, but I tell you" (5:21–22, 27–28, 31–32, 33–34, 38–39, 43–44). This is not meant to contradict his earlier compliance with the Law and Prophets, but to sharpen their ethical focus. For instance, they were instructed not to murder. "But I tell you that anyone who is angry with his brother will be subject to judgment" (5:22).

"Therefore, if you are offering your gift at the altar and there remember that your brother has something against you, leave your gift there in front of the altar. First go and be reconciled to your

---

4. Hare, *op. cit.*, 43.

The Golden Rule

brother; then come and offer your gift." Whether in this connection or some other, resolve matters promptly.

In like manner, they were not to commit adultery. "But I tell you that anyone who looks at a woman lustfully has already committed adultery in his heart" (5:28). This recalls the attractive wife of a former colleague. She made her way to the rear of the bus, accompanied by the approving gaze of a man seated in the front. Retracing her footsteps, she reprimanded him: "You should be ashamed of yourself." He slumped down into the seat, without saying a word.

Jesus next addresses a variety of related topics. "Be careful not to do your acts of righteousness before men, to be seen by them" (6:1). Otherwise, do not expect any further consideration.

"And when you pray, do not be like the hypocrites, for they love to pray standing in the synagogues and on the street corners to be seen by men" (6:5). Instead, petition your Father discreetly. And when you pray, do not babble like pagans, who think that God will hear them simply because of their insistence.

This, then, is how one ought to pray: "Our Father in heaven, hallowed is your name, your kingdom come, your will be done on earth as it is in heaven." Thus to cultivate our religious piety. "Give us today our daily bread. Forgive us our debts, as we also have forgiven our debtors. And lead us not into temptation, but deliver us from the evil one." Thus to fine-tune our inter-personal relationships.

Jesus then warns against making a public display of fasting. This leads to an admonition to lay up treasure in heaven, "where moth and rust do not destroy, and where thieves do not break in and steal." "Therefore," Jesus concludes, "do not worry about your life, what you will eat or drink, or about your body, what you will wear. Is not life more important than food, and the body more important than clothes?" (6:25). Consider the birds of the air, and the lilies of the field, how God providently provides for them.

"Why do you look at the speck of sawdust in your brother's eye and pay no attention to the plank in your own eye?" he rhetorically inquires (7:1). Such hyperbole was calculated to point out the inappropriateness of objecting to some trivial concern with another, while overlooking a much more grievous fault in oneself. Instead, remove the plank, and then be better able to cope with the speck.

"Ask and it will be given to you; seek and you will find; knock and the door will be opened to you" (7:7). For one who asks can be confident of receiving, one who seeks can expect to find, and one who knocks will find that the door will be opened. "Which of you, if your son asks for bread, will give him a stone?" "If you, then, though you are evil, know how to give good gifts to your children, how much more will your Father in heaven give good gifts to those who ask him!"

All things considered, "do to others what you would have them do to you" (7:12). Apart from its context, it allows for much that is unsavory. Given the fact that persons have not been schooled in Christian discipleship. Even with pertinent instruction, persons often settle for something less credible than the rigorous course of action set forth in the Sermon on the Mount.

"In one sense the Golden Rule represents the high point of the sermon. The four paragraphs that follow contrast the two ways (vv. 13–14), the two kinds of fruit (vv. 15–20), the two kinds of followers (vv. 21–23), and the two kinds of builders (vv. 24–27)."[5] This calls attention to the two ways exposed at the outset of the Psalms, and in accord with Jesus' extended observation: "for this sums up the Law and the Prophets."

In greater detail, "The *righteous* are those who choose God's way as opposed to their own. They do not negotiate life alone, whether from good intent or not, hoping for the best and inevitably falling short."[6] In Jewish commentary, they resist the evil inclination. In this regard, rabbi Akiba observed that it first resembles "a thread and at last it is like a rope of a ship."

As amply illustrated intent plays a critical role in moral behavior. With good intentions, we may reap favorable results. However,

---

5. Mounce, *op. cit.*, 67.
6. Inch, *Devotions with David*, 5.

The Golden Rule

this is not necessarily the case, since wise decisions complement good intentions.

"I should repeat from the outset that I do not think any one term or title fully captures the truth about the historical Jesus," Ben Witherington III admits. "But if we ask what heuristic category comes closest to explaining the most about who Jesus thought he was and what he said and did, what comes closest to explaining why early christological thinking about Jesus develops at it did, then we must come to grips with sages and Wisdom."[7] *The Golden Rule* when taken in context would seem to bear out this contention.

Several other observations could be mentioned in passing. The admonition to treat others as we would have them treat us obviously involves allowing for the integrity of persons, even when they forcefully disagree with us. This is manifest in the willingness to dialogue, in accord with Augustine's assertion: "All truth is God's truth." It goes without saying that not all that is said to be true is in fact true.

Conversely, we are obligated to speak the truth as we understand it in love (cf. Eph. 4:15). We are not to refrain, as if it were a matter of no consequence. Neither are we to speak harshly or vindictively.

We should be more disposed to dwell on their positive than negative con-siderations. This is in keeping with C. S. Lewis' observation that God is more inclined to employ carrots (incentives) than clubs. His precedent is applicable.

Furthermore, we ought to readily forgive those who offend us. Since we also are not above reproach. Moreover, we have been shown mercy.

Without equivocation, *The Golden Rule* also consists of a summons to wage warfare against the formidable forces of evil. "For our struggle is not against flesh and blood, but against the rulers, against the authorities, against the powers of this dark world and against the spiritual forces of evil in the heavenly realms" (Eph. 6:12). The idiom does not exclude the oppressive political

---

7. Witherington III, *The Jesus Quest: The Third Search for the Jew of Nazareth*, 185.

and social protagonists, but alerts us to the fact this resistance extends into the spiritual realm.

In conclusion, it could be said that the rationale implies, "Expect great things from God." This no less extends to its corollary, "Endeavor great things in his name."

4

In Christ

PAUL'S SIGNATURE EXPRESSION *IN Christ* has profound ethical implications. This will become increasingly evident as the discussion develops. Furthermore, it will provide a fitting conclusion to this initial segment of the text—dealing with select biblical themes.

Briefly stated, "'In Christ' the old ends and the new—a new creation—begins. The crucified and risen Christ is the divine agent of universal salvation, the divider of history into aeons, that 'no longer' aeon when all things were 'old' and the 'now' aeon when all things have become, and are, 'new.'"[1] Consequently, the stakes have greatly risen.

An inductive approach proves most inviting, recalling an earlier study I did along this line.[2] This will help avoid the temptation of dealing with broad generalities. It will also allow for the general classifications of Pauline correspondence: early, general, prison, and pastoral epistles.

Early Epistles. Galatians first solicits our attention. Controversy surrounds the occasion in which the epistle was composed. Whether before or after the Jerusalem Council—recorded in Acts 15,

---

1. Barnett, *The Second Epistle to the Corinthians*, 298.
2. Inch *In Christ and On Track*, 1–12.

and meant to address the obligations concerning Gentile converts. It was a serious matter, having created bitter antagonism and uncertainty.

Worthy of note, Paul first employs the designation *in Christ* in a corporate setting. "I was personally unknown to the churches of Judea that are in Christ," he observes (1:22). We are thus alerted to the fact that the call to follow Christ eventuates in community. Upon embracing him, we discover others of like precious faith. Even if isolated from others, we are aware of their presence and concern on our behalf.

This also provides a subtle reminder that there were churches scattered elsewhere. Such would reflect a range of cultural preferences. It would, in turn, serve as evidence that God delights in constructive diversity, as over against strict conformity.

The polemic builds: "We who are Jews by birth and not 'Gentile sinners' know that a man is not justified by observing the law, but by faith in Jesus Christ. So we, too, have put our faith in Christ Jesus that we may be justified by faith in Christ and not by observing the law, because by observing the law no one will be justified" (2:15–16). Three times the apostle sets *observing the law* over against twice being *justified by faith in Christ*.

The law, nonetheless, serves a constructive purpose. First, it points out God's uncompromising standards. Second, it painfully reminds us of our failure in this regard. "All have sinned and fall short of the glory of God," Paul concludes elsewhere (Rom. 3:23). Finally, it serves as a means to tutor us to Christ. As children, we were subject "to guardians and trustees until the time set by his father. But when the time had fully come, God sent his Son, born of a woman, born under law, to redeem those under law, that we might receive the full rights of sons" (Gal. 4:2, 4).

In summary, the apostle declares: "For in Christ Jesus neither circumcision nor uncircumcision has any value" (5:6). In graphic terms, the playing field has been leveled.

Our attention shifts to the Thessalonian epistles. Paul's ministry in Thessalonica was productive—especially among God-fearing Gentiles, before opposition forced him and Silas to take their

In Christ

leave. Now Timothy arrived with what was essentially a favorable progress report.

"For you, brothers, became imitators of God's churches in Judea, which are in Christ Jesus," Paul admonishes his readers (1 Thess. 2:14). In particular, since they had per-severed in the face of persecution. As previously allowed, they had experienced *the suffering of Christ*—as an extension of his ministry.

They, moreover, derived consolation in the process. Being aware that Christ was interceding on their behalf, and resulting in abounding grace. They also anticipated his promised return, and comprehensive provision for their needs.

"Brothers," Paul approvingly addresses them, "we do not want you to be ignorant about those who have fallen asleep, or to grieve like the rest of men, who have no hope" (1 Thess. 4:13). For they will be caught up to meet the Lord in the air, and so they—along with those still living will be with him forever.

"Be joyful always," the apostle concludes: "Pray continually; give thanks in all circumstances, for this is God's will for you in Christ Jesus" (1 Thess. 5:16). *Be joyful always*, since this is God's will for you in Christ; pray *continually*, for this is also God's will for you in Christ; and *give thanks in all* circumstances, for this is no less God's will in Christ. With such in mind, we take leave of Paul's early correspondence.

Major Epistles. The apostle's major epistles include First and Second Corinthians and Romans. Paul had spent a considerable time in the commercial center of Corinth. He now received a letter requiring a response. He was also troubled by reports he had received from independent sources. These revealed division and contention within the fellowship.

"To the church of God in Corinth, to those sanctified in Jesus Christ and called to be holy," he prefaces his remarks (1 Cor. 1:2). While we might have thought that a person so focused on justification would have taken little notice of sanctification, this proves not to be the case. Not only does the apostle draw attention to our relationship to God—as cultivated by faith, but its practical working out in consort with others. Consequently, one would conclude that he thought of those *in Christ* as manifestly works in progress.

"I always thank God for you because of his grace given you in Christ Jesus," the apostle subsequently confides (1:4). *Grace* consists of unmerited favor. "Amazing grace!" John Newton exclaims, "how sweet the sound that saved a wretch like me!"

"It is because of him (God) that you are in Christ Jesus," Paul adds (1:30). It is something we could not have imagined, let alone deserve. In this regard, C. S. Lewis observed: "That is one of the reasons I believe Christianity. It is a religion you could not have guessed. If it offered the just the kind of universe we had always expected, I should feel we were making it up."[3]

"We are fools for Christ," the apostle allows, "but you are so wise in Christ!" (4:10). *We are fools* in the sense of enduring ridicule, while endeavoring to disciple others. *You are wise* in a satirical sense, saying one thing while imply its opposite.

Employing hyperbole, "Even though you have ten thousand guardians in Christ, you do not have many fathers, for in Christ Jesus I became your father through the gospel" (4:15). The analogy is apropos.

"The grace of the Lord Jesus be with you," the apostle characteristically concludes. "My love to all of you in Christ Jesus. Amen" (16:23-24). *Grace* since it is by this means that they embrace and sustain life in Christ, and *love* as an assurance of his genuine concern.

Paul continued to monitor the situation at Corinth, resulting in additional correspondence. "But thanks be to God," he rejoices, "who always leads us in triumphant procession in Christ and through us spreads everywhere the fragrance of the knowledge of him" (2 Cor. 2:14). What he has been saying up to this point in the letter could be taken as a rather depressing account of his ministry. As if to balance this somewhat negative feature, Paul describes how God has without exception enabled him to carry on an effective ministry.

"We have been speaking in the sight of God as those in Christ," the apostle adamantly concludes, "and everything we do,

---

3. Lewis, *Mere Christianity*, 41-42.

dear friends, is for your strengthening" (12:19). Whether through encouragement or criticism, that they might be the beneficiary. And not them alone, but those they shall be privileged to serve.

Paul had long hoped to visit the believers in Rome, but was hindered by some pressing matter or another (cf. Rom. 1:13). He, nonetheless, continued to remember them in prayer, anticipating that he would soon be able to make the journey. While separated by distance, they were bonded together *in Christ*.

"This righteousness from God comes through faith in Jesus Christ to all who believe" (3:22). So while all have sinned, persons may be "justified freely by grace through the redemption that came by Christ Jesus." The term *redemption* occurs primarily in the Pauline correspondence, and implies the paying of a ransom.

"For the wages of sin is death, but the gift of God is eternal life in Christ Jesus our Lord" (6:23). Here *sin* and *the gift of God* are set over against one another. We are called upon to choose between them.

"Do not think of yourselves more highly than you ought, but rather think of yourself with sober judgment, in accordance with the measure of faith God has given you," the apostle cautions. "Just as each of us has one body with many members, and these members do not all have the same function, so in Christ we who are many form one body" (12:3–5). As for apt commentary, "Measurement by our own standards tends to result in a superiority complex, while measurement by the stands of others lead to an inferiority complex. Faith, on the other hand, always holds two things before the believers: we are sinners, but we are being redeemed by grace."[4]

The apostle eventually reached Rome as a prisoner, having appealed his case to Caesar. He remained there for an extended time while under house arrest. It appears that he was released, apprehended again and executed. If this is an accurate reconstruction, his prison epistles would likely have been written during his first imprisonment.

Prison Epistles. The prison epistles consist of Colossians, Ephesians, Philippians, and Philemon. Paul wrote to the Colossians

---

4. Edwards, *Romans*, 286.

concerning a false teacher, who constituted a threat to the church. "Basically, Paul is telling them that Christ has defeated the evil doers by his death on the cross (2:15). This means that the false teaching and enslaving regulations that come from human wisdom and from the ruling spirits of the universe (2:8) have no authority over the believers (2:10)."[5]

"We always thank the Father of our Lord Jesus Christ, when we pray for you," the apostle appreciatively writes, "because we have heard of your faith in Christ Jesus and of the love you have for all the saints" (1:3–4). *Faith* and *love* are thus coupled together in a cherished legacy: *faith* that what was preached to them was in fact true, and *love* as an evidence that God had begun a good work in them.

"We proclaim him (Christ, the hope of glory)," the apostle continues, "admonishing and teaching everyone with all wisdom, so that we may present everyone perfect in Christ" (1:28). Accordingly, *hope* is added to *faith* and *love* as features of life exper-ienced *in Christ*.

Paul's letter to the Ephesians is thought to be a general epistle, meant to expound on the Christian legacy. "Praise be to the God and Father of our Lord Jesus Christ," he enthusiastically approves, "who has blessed us in the heavenly realms with every spiritual blessing in Christ" (1:3). *Spiritual blessings* are likely meant to be distinguished from material blessings: such as forgiveness, the indwelling Spirit, and the hope of glory.

"In him we were also chosen," Paul confidently continues, "having been predestined according to the plan of him who works out everything in conformity to his will, in order that we, who were the first hope in Christ, might be for the praise of his glory. And you also were included in Christ when you heard the word of truth, the gospel of your salvation (1:11–13). All this has resulted from God's gracious orchestration.

"Be kind and compassionate to one another," the apostle admonishes, "forgiving each other, just as in Christ God forgave you" (4:22). *Forgiven in Christ*, they should be prone to *forgiving in Christ*. Otherwise, their witness lacks credibility.

---

5. Patzia, *Ephesians, Colossians, Philemon*, 7.

In Christ

"If then any comfort in Christ, if any consolation of love, if any fellowship with the Spirit, if any compassion and pity," Paul implores the Philippians, "fulfill my joy, that you be like-minded, having the same love, being one in spirit and purpose" (2:1–2). Since the former is manifest, then the latter should be forthcoming.

"And my God will meet all your needs according to his glorious riches in Christ Jesus," Paul assures his readers. "Greet all the saints in Christ Jesus" (4:19, 21). He speaks from experience.

The apostle also writes a letter to Philemon concerning a runaway slave named *Onesimus*. He urges that the fugitive be taken back as a beloved brother in the Lord. "Therefore, although in Christ I could be bold and order you to do what you ought to do, yet I appeal to you on the basis of love" (v. 8). Paul thus enjoins Philemon on the basis of a common faith *in Christ*.

Pastoral Epistles. The pastoral epistles embrace First and Second Timothy, along with Titus. "While the title is not technically quite correct in that the Epistles do not deal with pastoral duties in the sense of the care of souls, yet is popularly appropriate in denoting the essentially practical nature of the subject matter as distinguished from the other Epistles attributed to Paul."[6]

Timothy was a youthful associate of the apostle. "Don't let anyone look down on you because you are young," Paul admonishes him, "but set an example for the believers in speech, in life, in love, in faith and in purity" (1 Tim. 1:4). In this regard, demonstrate that you are spiritually mature beyond your years.

Titus was also actively engaged in the ministry, as a companion of Paul and Timothy. He, likewise, is described as "my true son" (Titus 1:4). His duties seem to have been of a more general nature. For instance, the apostle enjoins him: "Remind the people to be subject to rulers and authorities, to be obedient, to be ready to do whatever is good, to slander no one, to be peaceable and considerate, and to show true humility toward all men" (3:1). Whether in the regard or some other, cultivate all that is consistent with being *a new creation in Christ*.

---

6. Guthrie, *The Pastoral Epistles*, 17.

"The grace of our Lord was poured out on me abundantly," the apostle allows, "along with the faith and love that are in Christ Jesus" (1 Tim. 1:14). *Faith* and *love* parallel *goodness* and *love* in the Psalms (cf. 23:6). As such, they resemble two guard dogs, who protect the sheep from harm.

"Those who have served well gain an excellent standing and great assurance in their faith in Christ Jesus" (3:13). They benefit in two regards: their reputation is enhanced, and they derive confidence. Furthermore, we are assured that it is better to serve than to be served.

"Paul, an apostle of Christ Jesus by the will of God," he prefaces his second epistle to Timothy, "according to the promise of the life that is in Christ Jesus" (1:1). He thus affirms his apostolic office, by way of soliciting their faithful compliance. Such is meant to foster *the promise of the life that is in Christ Jesus*.

"What you have heard from me, keep as the pattern of sound teaching, with faith and love in Christ Jesus" (1:13). This contrasts to the false teaching they have received from those who deviate from the apostolic faith. *Faith* and *love* again appear in context of being *in Christ*. When lacking, their profession is suspect.

"You, then, my son, be strong in the grace that is in Christ Jesus. And the things you have heard me say in the presence of many witnesses entrust to reliable men who will also be qualified to teach others" (2:1). *Grace* is employed in the instrumental sense, recalling his confident assertion: "I can do all things through him who gives me strength" (Phil. 4:13).

"Therefore (since God's word remains unfettered) I endure everything for the sake of the elect, that they too may obtain the salvation that is in Christ Jesus, with eternal glory" (2:10). What did this entail? "I have worked much harder (than others who claim to teach the truth), been in prison more frequently, been flogged more severely, and been exposed to death again and again" (2 Cor. 11:23). In greater detail, "Five times I received from the Jews the forty lashes minus one. Three times I was beaten with rods, once I was stoned, three times I was shipwrecked." In conclusion,

In Christ

"Besides everything else, I face daily the pressure of my concern for all the churches."

So that others may be the beneficiaries of salvation *in Christ*. In this connection, Jesus declared: "I have come that they may have life, and have it to the full" (John 10:10). So that they may enjoy things held in common with others to a greater degree, and derive special blessing from a privileged relationship *in Christ*. We are thus alerted to the fact that *eternal life* exhibits a qualitative dimension.

On the other hand, "everyone who wants to live a godly life in Christ Jesus will be persecuted" (3:2). As a natural consequence, while not to the same degree (cf. 1 Peter 4:12–13). Hence, not something to be sought after but endured.

"We have thus seen that the expression *in Christ* embodies rich and varied nuances. It is sometimes employed in the context of personal devotion; in other instances, regarding life together; on still other occasions, in anticipation of the future."[7] Whether implicit or explicit, it appears never far from Paul's reasoning.

"It, moreover, is used to encourage believers in the face of relentless opposition and merciless persecution. Then as a means of consolation at the loss of a loved one. In subtle ways, such as a simple greeting. All things considered, as a constant point of reference in the midst of changing circumstances."[8]

---

7. Inch, *In Christ and On Track*, 11–12.
8. Ibid., 12.

II

Divine Mandates

5

Church Mandate

ETHICS DOES NOT FUNCTION in a social vacuum. Instead, it is associated with what has traditionally been designated as *divine mandates*. In this regard, "The authorization to speak is conferred from above on the Church, the family, labor, and government, only so long as they do not encroach upon each other's domains and only so long as they give effect to God's commandment in conjunction and collaboration with one another and each in its own way.[1]

Two qualifications are noted above. First, none of the institutions resulting from a divine mandate usurp divine sovereignty. As such, they are imperfect means for achieving God ultimate purposes.

Second, these must take care not to infringe on the legitimate domain of one another. Accordingly, they are not meant to compete, but to cooperate. Needless to say, they will be held appropriately accountable.

The *Church* first invites our consideration. "The Christian church was founded upon a story of a people's experience with Jesus and a vision of God's reign in human history. Throughout the

---

1. Bonhoeffer, *Ethics*, 279.

church's history this story has formed and transformed, sustained and changed the community's faith and life."[2]

This results in a privileged corporate memory concerning salvation history. Persons outside the fellowship characteristically retain a more limited recollection, not uncom-monly distorted by other influences. Even those within the circle of faith are not altogether immune from alien influences.

Then, too, Christians are drawn toward the future—in anticipation of Christ's return in glory. Qualifications aside, the past is prologue. Yes and the best is yet to come, although even now believers enjoy an earnest of that which is to come.

To live is to change, and the followers of Jesus courageously affirm life. Still, the more some things change, the more other features remain constant. Consequently, change in itself is not a virtue, but only insofar as it affirms abiding truth.

This recalls a graphic illustration. I observed that Korean churches did not appear as a rule to follow the cultural architecture evident elsewhere. When I inquired about this, I was told that the intent was to make them more visible. Now whether this was a wise decision or not, I cannot say. But one thing is certain, it was a calculated decision intended to achieve a legitimate goal.

As implied above, it is for the followers of Jesus to accommodate the church mandate. Christ summons them into community. In this capacity, they are—individually and collectively—meant to heartily respond to divine initiatives. This, in turn, requires constant vigilance.

For instance, a certain congregation set in place a procedure whereby it might minister more effectively in its community. Individual members were encouraged to submit recommendations. One concerned providing a legal service for persons in need. Another consisted of opening a Christian bookstore. These and other proposals were then prayerfully evaluated, and certain of them given priority. Funds were made available on a select basis, and as a rule repaid over a period of time.

---

2. Westerhoff III, *Living the Faith Community*, 27.

Church Mandate

Then, too, persons should be available to minister to one another. This might be done on an individual basis, through corporate means, or some combination of the two. If individually, it requires that persons be sufficiently aware of the needs of others, or in response to some request.

If through corporate means, one congregation instituted a lay program for pastoral ministry. Those participating were provided with a list of families they agreed to shepherd. They faithfully monitored church attendance as an indication of spiritual vitality, and were disposed to make telephone calls and home visits in line with their ministry.

Those outside the fellowship are implicated in a less direct manner. Initially, in that they recognize the integrity of the Christian community to fulfill its appointed task. This involves that which pertains to *coming apart* as a distinctive entity, and *going forth* in ministry. As for the former, to meet together for worship and instruction. As for the latter, an opportunity to herald the gospel and provide a holistic ministry.

The ideal is sometimes better served than others. Accordingly, we enjoyed the fellowship of Romanian Christians a few years after the collapse of the Communist regime. This had been an exceedingly difficult time, since the practice of the Christian faith was rigorously discouraged.

So it was that the sanctuary could no longer accommodate those attending. It was of no use to petition the authorities to allow for enlarging the edifice, since it would be denied. Under the cover of darkness, vehicles would arrive to carry off dirt excavated for the church extension, and disposed of elsewhere. Eventually a foundation was laid, but the officials supposed this was a playground and did not interfere.

Whereupon, the building began to take shape. Now alerted to the congregation's intent, the officials took the senior pastor into custody. Not wanting to make him a martyr, they deported him with the warning that if he should return, he would run the risk of being executed. Even so, they allowed the church extension to remain. This type of defiant activity came to be called the *Joshua Principle*, whereby the fellowship affirmed its church mandate prerogative.

The Church makes its presence felt in keeping with three concentric circles. Initially, in its distinctive capacity. *The Apostles' Creed* serves as a classic example. "I believe in God, the Father Almighty," it affirms at the outset. Since the creed serves as a corporate expression of faith, "we might expect it would begin with the first person plural—'We.' The use of the first person singular, however, proclaims the fact that no one else can believe for me."[3]

Believe pertains to a reasoned conviction. As such, it less resembles a leap in the dark than pressing on toward the light. It is in this manner that we are assured of things anticipated and not yet visible (cf. Heb. 11:1). As when "Noah, warned about things not yet seen, in holy fear built an ark to save his family" (v. 7).

God as *Father, Almighty* confirms his sovereign character. It brings to mind an occasion when I stopped by a shop in Bethlehem to visit an acquaintance. He was nowhere to be seen, but I heard the sound of muffled weeping from a corner of the room There I found the young man, curled up and sobbing. He had intended to emigrate to Canada, but when his father heard of it, he forbade his taking leave. He felt obligated to obey. In the memorable lyrics of John Sammis:

> When we walk with the Lord in the light of His Word,
> What a joy He sheds on our way!
> While we do His good will He abides with us still,
> And with all who trust and obey.

Secondly, there is recourse to para-church groups. These provide the luxury of taking a more definite stand on some issue. These are often along the line of some intermediate strategy to achieve illusive goals. As such, they enlist persons of similar persuasion.

They also attempt to work closely with the Church, while not pretending to speak for the Christian community as a whole. They thus testify to the willingness of Christians to deal with complex

---

3. Day, *The Apostles' Creed*, 13.

issues, and thereby avoid sins of omission. Whereupon, they qualify as a helpful adjunct, but not a legitimate substitute for the Church itself.

Finally, there are numerous opportunities for Christians to cooperate with other well-meaning persons. Such as providing for the needs of the poverty-stricken, services not readily available and emergency relief.

This need not compromise one's faith but readily enhances it. It bears repeating, "let your light shine before men, that they may see your good deeds and praise your Father in heaven" (Matt. 5:16). Whether via the Church, para-church, or voluntary association, may God receive his deserving glory.

Now the Church is said to manifest four attributes: unity, sanctity, catholicity (universality), and apostolic. However, it is apostolic in an instrumental sense. If apostolic, then one, holy, and universal. This precludes any alternative, such as ethnic, racial, or socio-economic identity.

Without equivocation, the Church is *apostolic*. Accordingly, "They devoted them-selves to the apostles' teaching and to the fellowship, of the breaking of bread and to prayer"(Acts 2:42). "The community, the apostolic fellowship, was constituted on the basis of the apostolic teaching. This teaching was authoritative because it was the teaching of the Lord communicated through the apostles in the power of the Spirit."[4]

For believers of later generations, the New Testament scriptures constitute the repository of apostolic teaching. These were considered normative for matters of faith and practice. As such, they were vigorously defended by the early church fathers against alien influences.

If apostolic, then resulting in *unity*. Not uniformity but constructive diversity. "The body is a unit, though it is made up of many parts, and though all its parts are many, they form one body" (1 Cor. 12:12). Although *a unit*, composed of *one body, it is made up of many parts*.

---

4. Bruce, *The Books of the Acts*, 73.

"Now you are the body of Christ, and each one of you is a part of it," Paul continues. "And in the church God has appointed first of all apostles, second prophets, third teachers, then workers of miracles, and those who have gifts of healing, those able to help others, those with gifts of administration and those speaking in different kinds of tongues" (vv. 27–28). Are all apostles? Obviously not. Are all prophets? Certainly not. Yet all foster Christian unity.

If apostolic, then also characterized by *sanctity*. This implies being set apart for God's service. As regards the temple: "Because of your temple at Jerusalem kings will bring you gifts" (Psa. 68:29). As concerns the chosen people, "Then you will remember to obey all my commands and will be consecrated for your God." (Num. 15:40). Thus whether pertaining to things or persons.

Accordingly, "But just as he who called you is holy, so be holy in all that you do" (1 Peter 1:15). Since God lived in the midst of his people, they "had to be holy, which meant in the first place cultic purity. But an examination of the context of the passages cited would show that the separated life-style was not simply cultic but also moral. God is a God of justice, and he cannot tolerate any form of evil and injustice."[5]

If apostolic, then finally *universal*. "Once, kneeling in the prairie sand of South-West Africa, I celebrated the Lord's Supper with some Herero tribesmen," Helmut Thielicke recalls. "Neither of us understood a single word of the other's language. But when I made the sign of the cross with my hand and pronounced the name 'Jesus' their dark faces lit up. We ate the same bread and drank from the same chalice, despite apartheid, and they couldn't do enough to show me their love."[6] Such speaks for itself.

Some years ago I was asked to participate in the ordination service of a youthful Nigerian pastor. At one point in the service the participants were encouraged to lay their hands on his head, while prayer was extended on his behalf. When I looked down, there were a number of relatively small black hands, and one larger white hand—my own. It was at that moment that I sensed

5. Davids, *The First Epistle of Peter*, 68–69.
6. Thielicke, *I Believe*, 231.

Church Mandate

as never before the awesome character of the church universal. It was sometime later when overhearing Billy Graham refer to the experience of becoming a *world Christian* that I could readily identify with it.

It remains to cite some random thoughts concerning the Church mandate. "On the basis of nearly all the images of the Church in Scripture," Avery Dulles concludes, "one is led to believe that the Church, far from passing away at the end of time, will then truly come into is own. In the preaching of Jesus, the Church is the little flock being led into heavenly pastures."[7] It thereby qualifies as an earnest of the future.

Jesus, however, alerted his disciples that an enemy had sown weeds among the wheat. These would be allowed to grow together until the harvest, when the two would be separated. At which time the weeds would be burned, and the wheat gathered in the barn (cf. Matt. 13:24–30, 36–43). Consequently, one needs to be discerning so as to appreciate the Church as an earnest of the consummation.

The church mandate is also portrayed as militant. "Finally, be strong in the Lord and in his mighty power," Paul cogently admonishes. "Put on the full armor of God so that you can take your stand against the devil's schemes. For our struggle is not against flesh and blood, but against the rulers, against the authorities, against the powers of this dark world and against the spiritual forces of evil in the heavenly realms" (Eph. 6:10–12). As previously noted, the idiom implies that the conflict involves not only political and social entities, but formidable spiritual adversaries.

In greater detail, "Stand firm then, with the belt of truth buckled around your waist, with the breastplate of righteousness in place, and with your feet fitted with the readiness that comes from the gospel of peace. In addition, to all this, take up the shield of faith, with which you can extinguish all the arrows of the evil one." Take also the helmet of salvation and the sword of the Spirit, which is the word of God, and coupled with unrelenting prayer.

"There is a subtle point that remains. The church in the abstract does not do justice to the church as one may experience it.

---

7. Dulles, *Models of the Church*, 104.

Mention of the church brings to mind a myriad of faces, such as would give rise to Paul's exaltation: 'I thank God every time I think of you' (Phil. 1:3)."[8]

I recall some of this *myriad of faces* from my childhood, even though I did not frequent church services. I remember others from my time in the military, when engaged in academic life, in overseas situations, and local churches. Then, too, seemingly in answer to some spiritual need. Thus the church mandate embraces a prized legacy.

---

8. Inch, *Why Take the Church Seriously?*, 131.

6

Family Mandate

THE FAMILY MANDATE PREDICTABLY brings to mind the saying, "The hand that rocks the cradle rules the world." We are thus reminded of the critical role the family plays in society. Here life is ideally conceived and sustained while the infant cannot fend for itself. "Train a child in the way he should go," the sage observes, "and when he is old he will not turn from it" (Prov. 22:6).

The pattern was set early on: "For this reason a man will leave his father and mother and be united with his wife, and they will become one flesh" (Gen. 2:24). So as to modify the former relationship insofar as it encumbers its replacement. Not as a means to weakening but enhancing the family structure.

"A man also must strive to prevent any dissolution of the relationship by clinging or cleaving (being *united*) to his wife. Clinging conveys commitment to maintaining the union in loyal love. In a relationship of mutual trust, a male and a female are free to be open and vulnerable to each other's presence."[1] Their commitment provides a secure setting in which to explore their God given sexuality.

It also precludes sexual intimacy outside of marriage. Whether before or subsequent to exchanging vows. Such as recalls David's

1. Hartley, *Genesis*, 63–64

indiscretion with Bathsheba, soliciting the rebuke of Nathan the prophet (cf. 1 Sam. 11–12). Then, in turn, leading to his earnest repentance.

Noted above, the family provides critical services—without which the child would not survive without an effective alternative. As is graphically expressed by breast feeding: "This is the period of the most intimate contact, almost a symbiosis between mother and child, a direct continuation of the prenatal mother-child unity, only one step removed from the marsupial young in the pouch."[2]

In her later years, my mother confided in me: "I can't remember that you ever did anything wrong." It would seem that love has a short memory, because I could recall innumerable instances.

The family also provides needed structure. "Chaos threatens our daily existence. Consequently, the family resembles a safe haven from the storms of life. As such, it cultivates a cherished sense of belonging."[3]

Here, within the family circle, there is order. There are familiar roles to play, and shared experiences. Accordingly, it brings to mind the Bedouin proverb: "I against my cousin, and my cousin and I against the stranger."

The family likewise addresses the need for self-esteem. Not only is it important to be accepted by others, but by oneself. Lacking in either regard, we have difficulty managing with the exigencies of life.

In ideal terms, one's parents convey God's concern for us. Created in his image, we are meant to have communion with him. Consequently, the lack of prayer seems not simply impious but unnatural. If for no other reason than being created in his image, this should greatly enhance our self-image.

Finally, the family assists us in self-actualization. In other words, to approach our potential. Moreover, in a distinctive manner. As sometimes expressed, "God wants creative originals instead of predictable copies." Not in isolation from those surrounding us, but in consort with them.

2. Patai, *The Arab Mind*, 30.
3. Inch, *Thumbs Up For The Family*, 1.

Family Mandate

As touched on earlier, this requires *hard love*—as over against permissiveness. It is in keeping with the sage saying, "Anything that is worth doing is worth doing well." Bearing in mind not only the immediate but long-term results. Consequently, there is much more at stake than we may realize at the moment.

The family in traditional Middle Eastern society is extended and patriarchal. It is usually supervised by an elderly male, its membership comprising "all his sons with their wives and children, and the unmarried daughters and granddaughters. The entire family resides together, in a cluster of neighboring tents in the nomadic camp, in a single house, or in several buildings clustered around a common courtyard in the villages and towns."[4]

Marriage within the extended family was preferred, since it enhances family solidarity. "Do not marry a Canaanite woman," Isaac enjoined Jacob. "Go at once to Paddan Aram, to the house of your mother's father Bethuel. Take a wife for yourself there, from among the daughters of Laban, your mother's brother. May God Almighty bless you and make you fruitful and increase your numbers until you become a com-munity of peoples" (Gen. 28:1–3).

The extended family also functions as an integral unity. In a nomadic tribe, its property is held in common; in the village, it owns jointly the land it cultivates; while in the towns it manages jointly the means by which they make a living. Earnings are as a rule shared, and expenses defrayed at the discretion of the patriarchal head.

Social conditioning is usually achieved informally. The children at a tender age participate in the work of their parents: the boys along with their father and/or older brothers, and the girls with their female counterparts. Girls, when they marry, at or frequently before puberty, are relocated with the family of their husband.

The nuclear family has largely come to replace the extended family in Western culture. It consists of father, mother, and children. It may also accommodate other family members, as the need arises. This recalls the time when my wife's elderly father came to

---

4. Patai, *Society, Culture, and change in the Middle East*, 21.

live with us. While commended by our friends for our self-sacrifice, my Nigerian students commented on how fortunate we were.

The mobile character of our industrial society promotes the nuclear family. Persons are inclined to pursue individual vocations, of their own choosing, and which will often require relocation. The extended family ties become strained in the process. As a result, the nuclear family enjoys relatively little support from other family members.

Parents, furthermore, have difficulty touching all bases. Since they must take on responsibilities previously assumed by other resident family members. This feature is intensified when both parents work outside the home, creating the *home alone* syndrome.

"It would appear that the nuclear family now has a serious rival in what, for lack of a better designation, I will call *the anonymous family*. It is a makeshift operation, calculated to provide needed services—in lieu of some better-defined alternatives. The single parent home serves as a prime example."[5] Strictly speaking, the single parent is not qualified to serve in the dual capacity of father and mother.

A recent study identified four family structures: stable intact, conflict intact, single parent, and stepfamily. Not surprising, the stable intact scored highest on the child well-being scale. Conversely, the single parent alternative scored lowest. While the conflict intact and stepfamily did better.

In greater detail, the single parent situation can embrace two or more generations of unmarried or divorced persons. While these may provide some of the advantages that accrue to the extended family, they do not usually provide the preferred male/female duality. The same sex liaison is even more problematic.

In another context, urban street children sometimes band together for mutual support. This can involve living accommodation, shared income, and mutually agreed upon rules of behavior. Whether this qualifies as a family or not, it provides some of the services we normally associate with a family.

---

5. Inch, *Thumbs Up For the Family*, 4.

Family Mandate

In still a different context, hospice care provides essential services once contributed by the family. This may serve in conjunction with, or in place of family involvement. Each instance is in some ways unique.

These illustrations will perhaps suffice to document that the traditional family is no longer as pervasive as an institution, other means having been devised to provide essential services. However, we should not, allow this to obscure the critical importance of the family mandate. As expressed by Pope Paul VI: "Marriage is not, then, the effect of chance or the product of evolution of unconscious natural forces; it is the wise institution of the Creator to realize in mankind His design of love."[6]

We now focus our attention to the marriage ceremony, as a means of elaborating the notion of family as mandate. The bride is commonly adorned in white, symbolic of chastity, and the groom in formal attire—while the attendants provide their encouragement. The father of the bride awaits his cue to present her on behalf of her mother and himself in marriage. The sanctuary accommodates family and friends.

"Dearly beloved," the cleric begins to read from the liturgy, "we are gathered together here in the sight of God, and in the face of this company, to join this Man and this Woman in holy Matrimony." While most are familiar with these words, few stop to reflect on their implications as a family mandate.

If *in the sight of God*, then to invoke his blessing. This would traditionally involve the birthing of children, considered an evidence of divine favor. However, it would extend to all facets of life. Good times and bad, labor and rest, when apart from one another and when together. Along with the confidence, "And we know that in all things God works together for the good of those who love him, who have been called according to his purpose" (Rom. 8:28).

Not only in God's presence, but along with *this company*. Marriage is not simply a religious but social contract. In traditional societies, it often signaled the alliance between two extended families. In any case, the couple was thus reminded of their obligation

---

6. Pope Paul VI, *"Humane Vitae,"* 8.

to their respective families. This also served to discourage divorce, since it had wider implications.

This man and this woman envisages a monogamous heterosexual union. As for the monogamy, exceptions were relatively rare in antiquity. As in the case when the wife failed to bear children. So it came to pass that Sarai encouraged Abram: "Go, sleep with my maidservant; perhaps I can build a family through her" (Gen. 16:3). As for a heterosexual union, marriage was associated with procreation.

In perfunctory manner, the cleric allows: "If any man can show just cause, why they may not lawfully be joined together, let him now speak or else hereafter forever hold his peace." There are legitimate reasons for objection. "For every one is not to marry, nor always," Clement of Alexandria cautions. "But there is a time in which it is suitable, and a person for whom it is suitable, and an age up to which it is suitable."[7]

The clergyman next turns his attention to the couple, directing them to reveal any reason why they cannot lawfully be joined in marriage. First, in that the hidden things will be disclosed in the Day of Judgment. Second, that if joined together otherwise than as God's word allows, their marriage is not valid.

Calling the man by his given name, the cleric inquires of his intention to have this woman to be his wife, "to live together after God's ordinance in the holy estate of Matrimony? Will you love her, comfort her, honor, and keep her in sickness and in health; and, forsaking all others, keep only unto her, so long as you both shall live?" The bride is then asked to give her consent. Marriage thus manifestly involves commitment.

"Who gives this Woman to be married to this Man?" the clergyman then inquires. As noted earlier, the father usually responds on his behalf and that of his wife.

Having dealt with the matter of intent, the couple are asked to repeat their vows—the groom first and then the bride. "Will you have this Woman/Man to be you're wedded Wife/Husband, to have and to hold from this day forward, for better for worse, for

---

7. Clement of Alexandria, *op. cit.*, II, xxiii.

richer for poorer, in sickness and in health, to love and to cherish, till death do us part, according to God's holy ordinance; and thereto I pledge you my love."

The exchange of rings is a common feature of wedding ceremonies. The wearing of rings was common in antiquity, both by men and women. While usually a matter of adornment, it might symbolize authority. In this instance, they serve as a token exchange of loving devotion.

Prayer is an integral feature of the marriage ceremony. As an example and in abbreviated form: "send your blessing upon these your servants, this man and this woman whom we bless in your Name; that these persons may surely perform and keep the vow and covenant between them and may ever remain in perfect love and peace together, and live according to your laws, through Jesus Christ our Lord. Amen." God is hereby depicted as a gracious benefactor. As if to confirm this impression, "Every good and perfect gift is from above, coming down from the Father of the heavenly lights, who does not change like shifting shadows" (James 1:17).

In the light of God's anticipated blessing, the couple is enjoined to keep the marriage covenant. Meanwhile, they are admonished to abide by God's irrevocable *laws*. This pertains to his *teaching*, which becomes binding on his subjects. Once again, we are reminded of the mandate structure of the family.

The ceremony closes with the declaration: "What God has joined together let no man put asunder." Given the sanctity of marriage, it comes as no surprise that both Judaism and Christianity consider divorce a tragic event. "As it says in the Talmud, 'When a man puts aside his wife of his youth, even the very altar weeps.' But Judaism is nothing if not realistic and recognized from its earliest days that divorce would happen; although marriage is holy, a deeply unhappy marriage is not holy."[8]

The declaration concludes: "Forasmuch as given name and given name have consented together in holy wedlock, and have witnessed the same before God and this company I pronounce

---

8. Robinson, *Essential Judaism*, 170.

that they are Man and Wife. In the Name of the Father, and of the Son, and the Holy Ghost. Amen." Since the conditions have been met and attested to by God and man, the marriage is officially recognized. Herewith we are assured of the mandate character of the family.

7

Labor Mandate

THE LABOR MANDATE EMERGES in various biblical contexts. In this regard, "The Lord God took the man and put him in the Garden of Eden to work it and take care of it" (Gen. 2:15). "It should be noted that even before the fall man was expected to work; paradise was not a life of leisured unemployment. Both *Enuma elish* and the Atrahasis epic also speak of man being created to work to relieve the gods. But the biblical narrative gives no hint that the creator is shuffling off his load onto man: work is intrinsic to human life."[1] "If I were hungry I would not tell you," the oracle protests, "for the world is mine, and all that is in it" (Psa. 50:12).

Man is thus encouraged to find fulfillment in his labor. This can be accomplished in several ways. For instance, by focusing on the service rendered to others. Accordingly, my father drew satisfaction from being able to support his family without enlisting the help of his offspring. In our village culture, a person was commended for being *a good provider*.

In addition, one can derive satisfaction from doing something well. My brother was meticulous in carrying out his duties. This seemed to meet a felt need. Meanwhile, his attention was not diverted by other matters.

1. Wenham, *Genesis 1–15*, 67.

Then, too, creativity is especially inviting. This allows us to identify in some measure with the divine Creator, who is usually depicted in traditional accounts as a celestial potter. Accordingly, creation was periodically described as *good*, and in the end *very good*. That is to say, it was both functional and aesthetically pleasing.

Needless to say, we no longer encounter work in its pristine form. "Cursed is the ground because of you," the Lord informed Adam, "through painful toil you will eat of it all the days of your life. It will produce thorns and thistles for you, and you will eat the plants of the field. By the sweat of your brow you will eat your food until you return to the ground, since from it you were taken, for dust you are and to dust you will return" (Gen. 3:17–19).

The same term for *pain* is used concerning both man and woman. "God placed pain for males and females at the center of the human effort to sustain life. This pain counters the arrogance that motivates humans to build a society apart from God. It also continually reminds humans of their limitations, mortality, and alienation from and dependence on God."[2] It thus serves a constructive purpose.

With the passing of time, the Israelites are engaged in forced labor. "Come," Pharaoh enjoined his subjects, "we must deal shrewdly with them or they will become even more numerous and, if war breaks out, will join our enemies, fight against us and leave the country" (Exod. 1:10). So they installed *slave masters*, "to oppress them with forced labor." It is said that evil consists of good having gone wrong, and this serves as a case in point.

As confirmation, the Lord informs Moses: "I have indeed seen the misery of my people in Egypt. I have heard them crying out because of their slave drivers, and I am concerned about their suffering. So I have come down to rescue them from the hand of the Egyptians and to bring them up out of that land into a good and spacious land, a land flowing with milk and honey" (3:7–8). It would be an ideal alterative from a shepherding perspective.

So it came to pass that the Israelites assembled at Sinai to covenant with the Almighty. "Six days you shall labor and do all your

---

2. Hartley, *op. cit.,* 70.

Labor Mandate

work," they are instructed, "but the seventh day is a Sabbath to the Lord your God" (Exod. 20:9-10). The Sabbath is thus framed in context of the labor mandate.

One was not allowed to engage in labor at the expense of the Sabbath celebration. Otherwise, it would be to lose the perspective of labor as a mandate. An alternative is graphically described by the sociologist Peter Berger as living under a *sacred canopy*. In other words, living in God's world by his grace. Instead, one succumbs to the *law of the jungle*.

Neither is one to engage in observing the Sabbath at the expense of gainful activity. Accordingly, the rabbis insisted that one could not worship properly without having been diligent in his or her labors. Work is commendable if in context of stewardship. If not, it compounds the problem of our alienation from the Lord God, and estrangement from one another.

As touched on earlier, the sage admonished: "Go to the ant, you sluggard; consider its ways and be wise" (Prov. 6:6). I was introduced to work at an early age. In this regard, I was encouraged to pick up my toys and put them in a fabric-covered box. The overflow was deposited in a storage area. Nothing was left laying around.

Later on, I was delegated responsibility to carry wood for the kitchen stove, and draw water from the nearby well. These were ongoing tasks. They were in keeping with the notion that persons should not expect others to do for them what they were not willing to do for themselves.

My brother and I usually wiped the dishes. Mother thought we performed this task better than our sisters, who seemed content with the impression. Mother, however, assigned them other duties.

Our obligations continued to expand with age. My brother and I soon assumed the primary responsibility for our vegetable garden. It required planting, weeding, and carrying water from the river that flowed nearby. My brother was more conscientious, while I wanted to complete the task as soon as possible.

Nonetheless, "I drew satisfaction from being able to make a contribution. While modest in comparison to our parents' input, it served to share the workload. As a result, I was a better person than would otherwise have been the case."[3]

We were urged to choose our mentors carefully. On one occasion, my mother became exasperated with my oldest sister for her lack of enthusiasm. "Take after your grandmother Mix (who was a bundle of energy)," she suggested. Whereupon, my sibling replied that she did not want to emulate her maternal but paternal grandmother—who was much more laid back.

Our village neighbors as a rule earned their livelihood through working in the woods, and/or on a farm. The work hours were long and demanding. My sisters and brother trained as teachers. While my sisters found the vocation more to their liking, my brother concluded that he would rather dig ditches for a living—his complaint largely having to do with the parents of his students. He, nonetheless, fared much better as an instructor in the military. Such should suffice to illustrate how the labor mandate works out in concrete terms.

The current situation now invites our attention. "Torn out of a Christian context, the meaning of work has been distorted. Bereft of a vision of eternity and driven by an ever more acquisitive culture, many people have become obsessed with success in the here and now, resulting in a major shift in social priorities."[4] Since it generally takes several generations for cultural principles to be forged or lapse, we may assume that this is a textbook case in point.

Materialism has increasingly become the cultural norm. As cynically expressed by a friend, "The one with the most toys wins." Conversely, Paul repudiated those "who think that godliness is a means to financial gain" (1 Tim. 6:5). "But godliness with contentment is great gain," he counters. "For we brought nothing into the world, and we can take nothing out of it. But if we have food and clothing, let us be content with that. For the love of money is the root of all kinds of evil." Not possessions per se, but the inordinate desire for them.

3. Inch, *Thumbs Up For The Family*, 100.
4. Colson and Pearcey, *How shall We Live?*, 341.

Labor Mandate

As for a compelling rationale, *we brought nothing into this world*, and *we can take nothing out of it*. This is graphically expressed by the Latin proverb: "The last robe has no pockets." Given this situation, greed seems ill advised. We ought rather to be content with the necessities of life. Since the more we have, the more we want. And the more we search for ways to justify our avarice.

The apostle concludes in climactic fashion that *the love of money is the root of all kinds of evil*. "Both Jews and Greeks had long before come to realize the disastrous effects that avarice has on people's lives, and they expressed it in proverbs. Paul is simply citing a proverb as support for his contention that greed is a trap full of many harmful desires that lead to all kinds of sin."[5]

Then, too, the workplace may seem more inviting than putting up with noisy children and dirty laundry. Along with this, there is increasing evidence that institutional care is not a good substitute for resident parents. Thus our social structure begins to deteriorate whenever one of the mandates is distorted.

Life, nonetheless, may be said to consist of turning obstacles into opportunities. Consequently, "It is time for the church to reclaim this crucial part of life, restoring a biblical understanding of work and economics should be a frequent subject for sermons, just as it was during the Reformation, when establishing one's vocation was considered a crucial element in discipleship."[6] Such would presumably involve a biblical understanding of the mandate structure, along with appropriate application.

Churches may also play a critical role in helping persons get off welfare, and become constructive members of society. While government programs can impart needed skills, they often lack the moral integrity to inculcate the habits of reliability, industry, and family commitment. Seeking out the cooperation of faith-based agencies thus proves to be a matter of strategic importance.

In similar manner, churches can minister to those released from prison, and undergoing drug rehabilitation. First, by educating

---

5. Fee, *1 and 2 Timothy, Titus*, 145.
6. Colson and Pearcey, *op. cit.*, 392.

persons for the task. After that, by providing proper supervision. Thus to promote labor within its mandate setting.

"If a man will not work," Paul accordingly allows for the possibility, "he shall not eat" (2 Thess. 3:10). While it may have been that Paul originated the saying, "it was certainly he who made it part of the Christian view of labor. The concluding statement is not a statement of fact, 'he shall not eat,' but an imperative, 'let him not eat.' Paul is giving the clearest expression to the thought that the Christian cannot be a drone. It is obligatory for him to be a worker."[7] The apostle practiced what he preached. "We were not idle when we were with you," he aptly recalls, "nor did we eat anyone's food without paying for it. On the contrary, we worked night and day, laboring and toiling so that we would not be a burden to any of you" (vv. 7–8).

Conversely, "We hear that some among you are idle. They are not busy; they are busybodies. Such people we command and urge in the Lord Jesus Christ to settle down and earn the bread they eat" (v. 11). He is obviously employing a play on words to contrast earnest labor with meddling in the affairs of others. As popularly expressed, "They had too much time on their hands."

His *command* echoes the theme of labor as a mandate, while his urging springs from a pastoral concern. This is according to Christ's teaching, and as an evidence of their faithful devotion.

Earlier on, the apostle enjoined his readers: "Make it your ambition to lead a quiet life, to mind your own business and to work with your hands, just as we told you, so that your daily life may win the respect of outsiders and so that you will not be dependent on anybody" (1 Thess. 4:11–12). The tone of the text calls for them to be unrelenting in their quest.

While *lead a quiet life* implies tranquility, it does not condone inactivity. It is both possible and desirable to be active in Christian service, and concurrently to be at peace. Accordingly, not to be unduly concerned about what others think or silenced by their resolute opposition.

---

7. Morris, *The First and Second Epistles to the Corinthians*, 256.

Labor Mandate

The admonition to *mind their own business* has both positive and negative implications. As for the former, they were to be conscientious in their work, rather than seeking a life of ease. As for the latter, they were not to meddle in the affairs of others. A failure in either regard would leave them open to the charge of inconsistency.

The section dealing with earning one's living is closely associated with the previous segment concerning brotherly love. "Those who imposed on the generosity of their fellows were not living in love. Or, to put the same thing the other way around, the exhortation to brotherly love carries with it the necessity for providing for one's own needs, so that undue strain may not be placed on the brother."[8] *Love* and *labor* are thus coupled together in the context of discipleship.

Paul subsequently calls our attention to the relationship between slaves and masters, the nearest modern equivalent being employees and employers. "Slaves, obey your earthly masters with respect and fear, and with sincerity of heart, just as you would obey Christ. Obey them not only to win their favor when their eye is on you, but like slaves of Christ, doing the will of God from your heart" (Eph. 6:5–6).

Since many slaves had embraced the Christian faith, it is not surprising that they should be singled out for instruction. "For the majority of them, membership in the church may have been the only time and place they could experience equality and brotherhood. But belonging to Christ did not remove them from the world or lead to their emancipation."[9] Consequently, their position was in critical need for clarification.

"And masters, treat your slaves in the same way. Do not threaten them, since you know that he who is both their Master and yours is in heaven, and there is no favoritism with him" (6:9) Regardless of social status, all persons are equal in God's sight. Therefore, persons should treat one another with respect and compassion. Thus the labor mandate solicits our deliberate attention, and ready application.

---

8. Ibid., 134.
9. Patzia, *op. cit.*, 21.

8

Government Mandate

IT CAME TO PASS that the Pharisees and Herodians cooperated to discredit Jesus. As for the former, they seemed reluctant but willing to accept Roman occupation, providing it did not interfere with their religious practices. As for the Herodians, it would appear that they supported Herodian rule.

"Teacher," they inquired, "we know you are a man of integrity and that you teach the way of God in accordance with the truth. You aren't swayed by men, because you pay no attention to who they are. Tell us then, what is your opinion? Is it right to pay taxes to Caesar or not?" (Matt. 22:15–17). They meant to put Jesus on the horns of a dilemma. If he were to advocate the paying of taxes, he would lose support from the populace. If, conversely, he were to protest the paying of taxes, he might be charged with rebellion.

Jesus was quite aware of their intent. "You hypocrites," he rebuked them, "why are you trying to trap me? Show me the coin used for paying the tax." When they brought him a denarius, he inquired: "Whose portrait is this? And whose inscription?"

"Caesar's," they acknowledged.

Government Mandate

Whereupon, he enjoined them: "Give to Caesar what is Caesar's and to God what is God's." Having failed in their effort to trap Jesus, they withdrew.

It was not Jesus' intention to suggest that there were two equally valid spheres: the religious and the secular. Jewish tradition held that foreign rulers exercised control at God's discretion, as evidence of the failure of the chosen people to abide by their covenant obligations. In this capacity, they would be held compatible. Thus are we graphically introduced to the government mandate.

"All the above was obscure to me as a youngster. My first encounter with political activity revolved around the town meeting. It was a rather raucous affair. There were efforts at humorous rejoinder. Tempers flared. The business was eventually expedited."[1] For better and worse, the results lingered.

My involvement in political life has been modest. On one occasion, I was urged by the League of Women Voters to run for the school board. It was then decided that it was not its prerogative to publically endorse a candidate. Without visible support, I failed to win the election.

On another occasion, I enjoyed a cordial relationship with our state senator. This encouraged me to express my views on two pending pieces of legislation. He took issue with both of my opinions, while convincing me to change my mind in one of the two instances. We remained good friends.

Upon moving from the eastern coast to the Midwest, I was unprepared for the substantive shift in political ideology. Invited to attend the meeting of some political activists, I had never encountered such a conservative group, and was at a loss as how to interact. Incidentally, I have always considered myself as being somewhat right of center on the political continuum, in keeping with the general average.

In the course of my political journey, I came across what was for me a novel idea from the writing of Reinhold Niebuhr. He reasoned that the axiom *in but not of the world* could be viewed in a corporate setting. That is, while some Christians are called to

---

1. Inch, *Thumbs Up For the Family,* 117.

church related vocations, others are meant to focus their efforts on social and political affairs. When coupled together, this suggests a strategic posturing of the community of believers.

While parents should acquaint their offspring with vocational alternatives, the Church can also lend a helping hand. This would amount to expanding the current efforts to inform the congregation concerning the outreach of their missionaries, to include other church related vocations and those in the public realm.

"Apart from vocation, all should take their role as citizens in a participatory democracy seriously. This includes being well informed, expressing one's views as appropriate, and voting one's convictions. It no less invites prayer for those in positions of authority."[2] It goes without saying that one must take into consideration the political reality of a given situation.

The conflict between idealism—which is based on moral principles, and pragmatism—alternatively associated with expediency is difficult to resolve. Since both are matters of legitimate concern. In any case, my personal preference is for persons who think in terms of broad initiatives. This must be coupled with the ability to delegate responsibility, and hold persons accountable.

When Christians retreat from the political arena, they readily become an endangered specie. This was impressed upon me in the wake of World War II, primarily with regard to the provocative writings of Dietrich Bonhoeffer. Then in conversation with Professor Helmut Ziefle, who recalled his first-hand experiences as a youth in Nazi Germany.

The Nazi regime attempted to stifle the prophetic voice of the Church, as expressed by the so-called *Confessional Church*. Furthermore, it meant to reconstruct the Church along Arian lines. This was a relatively long-range undertaking, requiring subtle man-ipualtion. The fall of the Third Reich cut short its political agenda.

We now turn to several representative case studies, as a means of expanding on the topic. In this regard, Daniel Estes evaluates three modes for assessing political leadership. First he explores *the*

2. Ibid., 118.

pragmatic model—implied earlier. In this instance, one focuses on the results that are anticipated.

The problems with this approach are legion. For instance, hindsight is characteristically preferable to foresight. Furthermore, it is difficult to distinguish between what is simply expedient and a long-term resolution. All things considered, one is easily misled.

Second, Estes defers to *the integrity model*. This requires evaluating "the personal character of the political leader. If the leader has a commendable character, then he will be able to maintain a good role model for his constituents as he responds to the unpredictable challenges of office according to the patterns he has already established in life."[3]

This would seem to be a part truth at best. A certain politician, whom I would prefer not to identify, was an exceedingly devout individual. However, he struck me as being quite naive, compounding the problems with which he had to deal. Most would agree that he should have taken a more realistic approach to issues.

Finally, Estes alludes to *the values model*. "It reasons that over time the public conduct of the leader will be marked by his personal character, which reflects his values. Therefore, the focus of evaluation is placed upon the principle criterion by which the leader sees the world, for this is the integrative center of his life."[4]

While there is much to be said for this option, there is no guarantee that the implications of one's worldview will be aptly applied. Nor does it touch on the ability of the person to take decisive action, nor maintain his resolve in the face of unrelenting opposition. In conclusion, it would appear that one must make a judgment based on complex criteria, and subject to re-evaluation. Accordingly, welcome to the real world!

Citing another provocative article, D. Jeffrey Bingham expounds on how Irenaeus viewed government. According to Irenaeus' understanding, "the State exists as God's creation for the purpose of ordering justice by penalizing injustice. (He) also states

---

3. Estes, "Psalm 101 and the Ethics of Political Leadership," *God and Caesar*, 21.

4. Ibid., 21–22.

that God has established these human rulers in a manner that fits those who at any given time are under their rule. There is diversity within the activities of the rulers established by God."[5]

He manifestly charges public officials with fostering justice by reprimanding injustice. "Do you want to be free from fear of the one in authority?" Paul inquires in this regard. "Then do what is right and he will commend you. For he is God's servant to do you good. But if you do wrong, be afraid, for he does not bear the sword for nothing" (Rom. 13:3–4).

Additionally, he accents constructive diversity within the scope of God's benevolent purposes. Thus contrasting points of view may provide a more accurate assessment of issue. Then, too, this allows for the kind of political ferment that negotiates changing circumstances.

Bingham subsequently adds seven principles, derived from his reading of Irenaeus: (1) Human government exists through the ordination of God. (2) Christians are obligated to pay taxes to the government ordained by God. (3) Human government exists as a concession to humanity's refusal to fear God. (4) Human government exists as a means to benefit humanity through the structuring of justice. (5) The aims of human government to structure peace and justice are consistent with God's own benevolent, just nature and identity as Creator. (6) Human government conducts itself in diverse ways, both just and unjust. (7) Although human government exists by God's design as a concession to human rejection of God, in order beneficially to structure justice, it does not supplant God's own sovereign dispensing of universal justice. Whether through the just conduct of the magistrates or God's condemnation of their injustice, he still dispenses just judgment to all.[6]

Human government is thus portrayed as a divine mandate. As such, it is not without its shortcomings. Humans, being fallible, have mixed motives. So it is that when justice is perverted,

---

5. Bingham, "Irenaeus and the Kingdoms of the World," *God and Caesar*, 30, 32.

6. Ibid., 33; cf. Irenaeus, *Against Heresies*, V, 24, 1–3.

Christians must appeal to a higher authority, even when this involves personal risk.

Taking a more practical approach, Jay Stack explores the impact that voluntary service can have on social and political affairs. "The Bible says that without vision the people perish," he readily allows, "but I want to remind you that without people the vision will perish. In thinking about this conflict of vision, first of all, if we Christians are to make a difference in the arena of social issues, we must decide what issues we are going to emphasize."[7]

Without people the vision will perish. There will be a variety of persons, drawn from different circumstances, and engaging in different enterprises. Sometimes their awareness will build with the passing of time; on other occasions, it will dawn suddenly in the course of events. In any case, it must be cultivated.

Persons must decide which issues to emphasize. This decision is born of necessity, since our time is limited. In this connection, "As for man, his days are like grass, he flourishes like a flower of the field; the wind blows over it and it is gone, and its place remembers it no more" (Psa. 103:15–16).

A likely scenario is to adopt some issue by way of an inherited concern. For instance, my paternal grandfather owned a store located near an access between the United States and Canada. This was at a time when there were extensive illegal liquor sales across the border. Grandfather, as an outspoken critic, drew the ire of those involved. As a result, his store was burned and he removed his family to a safer environ. This, along with related events, was appreciatively recalled within the family circle, and as an incentive to social obligation.

Sometimes the decision is derived from more immediate concerns. "I am very, very grateful that my wife is very active in the crisis pregnancy center that our church sponsors," Stack observes. "I learned that it was one thing to preach against abortion, but it was another thing to be pro-life. I watched as we joined hands with some other denominations and came up with

---

7. Stack, "How Christians Can Have an Impact on Volunteers, *Citizens Christians*, 120.

a home for unwed mothers—not just a crisis pregnancy center, but a home. We had several hundred people in our church volunteer to help in the home."[8]

One person can make a decided difference. If not at once, then with the passing of time. If not by him or herself, then in league with others. The problem is that there are far too many persons sitting in the stands, while far too few are on the playing field.

"You want to know how Christian volunteers can change their society?" Stack rhe-torically inquires. "We can register folks to vote." He speaks from experience, and leads by example.

"We can be politically active," he adds. "We ought to be; it is a sin not to be." *Sin* amounts to any lack of conformity to God's righteous will. As such, it may be either a sin of commission or a sin of omission—and the latter is often more grievous.

"We can give." As noted earlier, the rabbis coupled generosity with industry. And again as cited previously, the genuine measure of generosity is not how much we give, but how much remains after having given.

"We can orchestrate." In other words, we can enlist people in a common task. After that, blend their gifts in a constructive enterprise. Moreover, strive for excellence.

"We can hand out leaflets." It requires little in the way of expertise. A winsome smile is a welcome attribute. Cultivated in one context, it can readily be extended in others.

"We can fight." As when arguing the merits of a case before the judiciary. In any case, recalling the sage observation: "All that is necessary for evil to triumph is for good people to do nothing."

"We can defend." Especially those who are most vulnerable. Restoring dignity to the downtrodden. Lifting up the fallen.

In conclusion, Stack allows: "To me a Christian volunteer is someone who knows, by the grace of God, that I'm going to cross the finish line. I just don't want to cross it by myself. I want to take someone with me." He implies that voluntary activity is contagious, and in keeping with the government mandate.

---

8. Ibid., 128–29.

III

Cardinal Virtues

9

Justice

WE TURN OUR ATTENTION from the divine mandates to the acquisition of virtue, and the *cardinal virtues* in particular—said to be foundational. In particular: justice, prudence, temperance, and fortitude. This exploration becomes imperative since man's fall has seriously compromised his moral integrity.

Justice first solicits our consideration. "Away with the noise of your songs!" the oracle exclaims. "I will not listen to the music of your harps. But let justice roll on like a river, righteousness like a never-failing stream!" (Amos 5:23–24). The intensity of the reproach is striking, in that the cluster of abhorrent practices accents the thoroughness of God's rejection of their ritual overtures.

While appropriate means of worship, they are inconsistent with a failure to promote *justice* and *righteousness*. "The similes were especially effective in a context where most streams were seasonal, abounding with life-giving water in the rainy seasons and bone-dry through the long, hot summer. A society in covenant with Yahweh could no more live without them than without an adequate and steady water supply."[1]

---

1. Hubbard, *Joel & Amos*, 182–83.

Justice is complex in character. For instance, there is *legal justice*. This recalls a true story. A conscientious police officer closed a bar which had exceeded its curfew. The case was postponed until a judge who could be bribed was on duty. Whereupon, he reprimanded the officer, and warned him under the penalty of being charged with unlawful entry should he again intervene.

The public servant was crestfallen. He deliberated whether to resign or tolerate the injustice inflicted by the magistrate. At last report, he was still undecided.

Of course, the quest for legal justice is not a new venture. In a classic instance, Solomon was called upon to adjudicate a matter concerning two prostitutes. "My Lord, this woman and I live in the same house," one of them allowed. "I had a baby while she was there with me. The third day after my child was born, this woman also had a baby. We were alone; there was no one in the house with us" (1 Kings 3:17–18).

"During the night this woman's son died because she lay on him," she continued. "So she got up in the middle of the night and took my son from my side while I your servant was asleep. She put him by her breast and put her dead son to my breast." Awakening the next morning, she discovered the deceased child. Looking more closely, she realized that it was not her son.

"No!" the other woman exclaimed. "The living one is my son; the dead one is yours." They continued to argue between themselves.

"Bring me a sword," the magistrate ordered his attendant. Whereupon, he ordered that the child be cut in two, so that each woman would receive half.

"Please, my lord, give her the living baby!" pled the true mother. "Don't kill him!"

"Neither I nor you shall have him," the other woman taunted her. "Cut him in two!" Then Solomon acknowledged the first woman as the legitimate mother. Justice was thus served, and the magistrate's wisdom acclaimed.

Justice

Several extended observations are in order. First, legal justice allows for no exceptions. Otherwise, the prostitutes might well have been neglected, since their vocation was frowned upon.

Second, each of the women was given a hearing. The decision would be rendered on pertinent evidence. Accordingly, so as not to show preference.

"Finally, the decision should be such as would solicit social approval. All too often this is not the case. Consequently mistrust and cynicism result. The situation is inclined to deteriorate."[2]

How long will you defend the unjust and show partiality to the wicked?" the oracle protests. "Defend the cause of the weak and fatherless; maintain the rights of the poor and oppressed" (Psa. 82:2-3). "We now detect the irony that the judges have now become the judged. More specifically, the administration of justice—in God's view—includes rescuing and delivering *the weak* and *the poor*."[3] Since these are most unlikely to be given proper consideration.

How long alerts us to the fact that injustice persists. Not simply in exceptional instances, but as prevalent. Once allowed to take root, it proves to be exceedingly difficult to eliminate.

"Among the people are wicked men," the prophet protests. "Their evil deeds have no limit; they do not plead the case of the fatherless to win it, they do not defend the rights of the poor" (Jer. 5:26, 28). The *wicked men* resemble social parasites. They seek by devious means to accumulate wealth and privilege. In the process, they subvert legal justice. "Shall I not punish them for this?" the Lord rhetorically inquires. Most assuredly!

Then there is *retributive justice*. In brief, the punishment should fit the crime (cf. Exod. 21:23-25). This was meant to prohibit excessive retribution. Conversely, there might be extenuating circumstances which would allow for a lesser sentence. In this regard, there were cities of refuge provided for those who had inadvertently killed another. Accordingly, "These six cities will be a place of refuge for Israelites, aliens and any other people living

---

2. Inch, *The Enigma of Justice*, 71.
3. Broyles, *Psalms*, 336.

among them, so that anyone who has killed another accidentally can live there" (Num. 35:15).

"You have heard it said, 'Eye for eye, and tooth for tooth,'" Jesus allowed—as noted earlier. "But I tell you, do not resist an evil person. If anyone smites you on the right cheek, turn to him the other also" (Matt. 5:38–39). Given the cultural setting, he probably had in mind being struck by the back of the hand, as a calculated insult. Even so, he advocated returning good for evil.

The wanton taking of life was strictly forbidden, under the penalty of execution. This pertained not only to the Israelites, but to those living among them. All alike were created in God's image and deserving of protection under the law.

Moreover, great care was to be exercised in order to assure that the charge was legitimate. Consequently, "On the testimony of two or three witnesses a man shall be put to death, but no one shall be put to death on the testimony of only one witness" (Deut. 17:6). This was meant to provide the means for *purging the evil among you.*

Qualifications aside, one's culpability extended to the injuries inflicted by his animals. In this connection, "If a bull gores a man or a woman to death, the bull must be stoned to death. But the owner of the bull will not be held responsible. If, however, the bull has had the habit of goring and the owner has been warned but has not kept it penned up and it kills a man or woman, the owner also must be put to death" (Exod. 21:28–29).

"If a man steals an ox or a sheep and slaughters it or sells it, he must pay back five head of cattle for the ox and four sheep for the sheep" (22:1).

If a thief is caught breaking in during the night, and is injured so that he dies, the defender is guiltless. If, however, it should happen after sunrise, he is culpable. Not only is there an obligation to make restitution, but should he be without the means to do so, he can be sold into slavery. This provides a means for reparation.

Social relations were likewise a critical concern. "If a man seduces a virgin, who is not pledged to be married and sleeps with her, he must pay the bride-price, and she shall be his wife. If her

Justice

father absolutely refuses to give her to him, he must still pay the bride-price for virgins" (22:16 –17).

Rehabilitation also plays a legitimate role in retributive justice. Accordingly, certain of the scribes and Pharisees brought Jesus an allegedly adulterous woman. "Teacher," they assured him, "this woman was caught in the act of adultery. In the Law Moses commanded us to stone such a woman. Now what do you say?" (John 8:5). "What they wanted to do was to put Jesus in a dilemma from which he could not escape. If he said to stone her he would violate the Roman law in pronouncing a death sentence without Roman authority. If he said to free her it would appear that he was soft on or ignoring the Mosaic Law."[4]

Then, too, if she had been caught in adultery, what had become of her partner? Since he was no less culpable. Whereupon, Jesus bent down and began writing in the sand. When pressed for a response, he replied: "If anyone of you is without sin, let him be the first to throw a stone at her." At this, her accusers began to take their leave, beginning at the eldest and leaving Jesus and the woman alone. "Woman," he respectfully addressed her, "where are they? Has no one condemned you?"

"No one, sir," she responded.

Then neither do I condemn you,' he replied. "Go now and leave your life of sin." Thus retributive justice attempts to negotiate the varied exigencies of life.

In addition, there is *commutative justice*. This has to do with the allocation and transfer of goods and services. It initially recalls my father, who owned a general store. He had reluctantly passed up an athletic scholarship in order to assist my grandfather in the business.

He put in long hours. During the winter months, this entailed rising early so as to build a fire in the furnace. When returning late in the evening, he wasted little time in making his way to the bedroom. Closed on Sunday, he would often accommodate per-sons who appealed to him.

---

4. Carter, *John*, 68.

Folk not uncommonly took advantage of him. When allowed to charge their purchases, they were often hesitant to reimburse him. They would shop elsewhere as a means of escaping their responsibility. Then, when pressed for assistance, they would plead for him to grant them more credit.

How well was justice served? Especially in that it dictates a fair return on services rendered. When depressed by his lot in life, my father would on occasion refer to the store as his *jail*. Conversely, he was seldom happier than when walking through a wooded area, where he felt closest to God.

Commutative justice first makes its appearance with Cain and Abel. "Now Abel kept flocks, and Cain worked the soil" (Gen. 4:2). Neither vocation appears intrinsically preferable to the other. One might suppose that they cultivated different perspectives concerning commutative justice. In the process, tensions would arise.

"In the course of time Cain brought some of the fruits of the soil as an offering to the Lord. But Abel brought fat portions from some of his firstborn of his flock. Consequently, the Lord looked with favor on Abel's offering, but not that of Cain. The reason being that while Abel brought a choice offering, such as one would provide for an honored guest, Cain settled for a token alternative.

Cain became exceedingly angry, and took the life of his younger sibling. We are thus alerted to the fact that issues related to commutative justice have wider implications. Accordingly, we do well to deal conscientiously with them.

We subsequently read that Jacob upon arriving in the vicinity of Shechem pitched his tent within sight of the city. "For a hundred pieces of silver, he bought from the sons of Hamor this plot of ground where he had pitched his tent" (Gen. 33:19). As with Abraham before him, he purchased this property as an earnest of the promised land.

This procedure would involve various social amenities. "For instance, one would suppose that he indicted his intent by initially pitching his tent. This initiative could be rejected, provided that there was no implied coercion, and the conditions for sale were

Justice

acceptable. Then, in addition, the agreement would act as a social contract, providing security for the participants."[5]

Now slavery was widespread in the ancient Near East, although the economy was not necessarily dependent on it. Slaves could be procured from their owners, merchants, prisoners of war, or simply as a solution to their indebtedness. In this regard, "If a fellow Hebrew, a man or a woman, sells himself to you and serves you six years, in the seventh year you must let him go free. And when you release him, do not send him away empty-handed. Supply him liberally from your flock, your threshing floor, and your winepress" (Deut. 15:14).

Accordingly, the Genesis narrative resembles an emancipation proclamation. So it was that the Jewish tradition concluded that as long as anyone remains in bondage, no one is genuinely free.

Furthermore, slavery exists in more subtle forms. As when the markets are manipulated to require that persons work inordinately long hours, with modest remuneration. Sometimes under duress, so that one is virtually driven to the brink of despair.

Commutative justice also requires that we give attention to detail. Accordingly, "You must have accurate and honest weights and measures, so that you may live long in the land the Lord your God is giving you" (Deut. 25:15). "Fair trade is one of the essential hallmarks of any human society seeking to protect everybody's interest in a civilized way. There is, on the one hand, the positive promise that commitment to honesty will bring the covenant while they were still in it. However, he concludes, we were wrong blessing."[6] There is, on the other hand, caution that dishonesty is *detestable* to the Lord.

Distributive justice finally solicits our attention. "Distributive justice regulates the measure of privileges, aids, burdens or charges, and obligations of the individual as a member of the community."[7] Consequently, a person exercises distributive justice by assuming

---

5. Inch, *The Enigma of Justice*, 57.
6. Wright, *Deuteronomy*, 250.
7. Haring, *The Law of Christ*, vol. 1, 517.

an appropriate obligation for society, while not insisting on excessive privileges.

Michael Bauman reflects on what he provocative identifies as *the dangerous Samaritan*, recalling the occasion when a scribe, wanting to justify himself, asked Jesus:

In this regard, he reasons that we thought we were doing the right thing when we passed laws to raise wages and lower rent, if we gave generously to help support single mothers, and aided the poor in their flight from poverty, and alleviated much of their distress while they were still in it. However, he concludes, we were wrong.[8]

In greater detail, good intentions are not adequate. First, we thought that if we passed laws mandating higher wages for the lowest paid workers, we could increase their income—thus helping them escape poverty. We failed to take into consideration that the lower paid workers are usually those with less skill and experience, and therefore less desirable. By artificially raising wages, we made them even less desirable.

Second, we thought that by legislating a reduction of cost for urban housing, we could make available less expensive accommodations. We ignored the fact that the more appealing to the renter, the less so to the owner. As a result, landlords decided to allocate their investments in other ways.

Third, we thought that by providing welfare for the mothers of illegitimate children, we would make life easier for them and their offspring. We overlooked the fact that this would actually encourage persons to perpetuate their reliance from one generation to the next. This resulted in what is graphically described as *a welfare state.*

Finally, by distributing funds among the poor, we thought it would simply provide a means of aiding and comforting the unfortunate. We failed to take into consideration that poverty itself might not be the problem, but only a symptom. In failing to speak to the deeper need, we thus compounded the problem.

---

8. Bauman, "The Dangerous Samaritan: how We Unintentionally Injure the Poor," *God & Caesar,* 201.

Worthy of note, "Christian love operates upon the premise that the defeat of poverty is a joint effort, or common endeavor, between the have and have nots, not an unilateral thrust by the haves only. The recipients of Christian charity ought to be either diligent workers or else unable."[9] In other words, there is a hierarchy of needs to be addressed.

Baumann concludes that in order to succeed, we must qualify as *good* rather than *dangerous* Samaritans. Accordingly, (1) Put our programs in the hands of contributors, rather than recipients or bureaucrats. As for the former, they are more inclined to make a genuine effort to alleviate the problem.

(2) Redefine poverty. Nearly 40 percent of those designated as *poor* own their own homes, with more living space than enjoyed by most middle class Europeans. Nearly 70 percent of America's poor own at least one car. Instead, poverty should pertain to the lack of food, shelter, or clothing.

(3) Re-educate the politicians and those designated as poor. Bring to their attention that welfare can be addictive and debilitating. Nor is it a shame to be poor; the shame lies in being slothful.

(4) No perfect solutions are possible. Poverty cannot be eradicated, only ameliorated. The bad news is that all our good intentions will fall short; while the good news is that the situation can be greatly improved.

(5) One should not demand special considerations, but settle for what is implied by *distributive justice*. This requires a cooperative endeavor, consideration of others, and righteous resolve. Then, too, good Samaritans are in great demand.

---

9. Ibid., 211.

10

Prudence

PRUDENCE IS ANOTHER OF the cardinal virtues. It implies sound judgment in practical matters. As such, it is closely akin to *wisdom*, although its focus tends to be more on specifics. It has also come to be associated with caution.

"Just as the artisan forges his sword or weaves a rug, so the sage tells us how to live life with finesse. He corrects those of us who blunder along, from one day to the next, saying the wrong thing, doing the wrong thing, wishing we could do better"[1] If given the opportunity, and then in a tactful manner.

A representative passage from Proverbs will serve to elaborate. "Do not withhold good from those who deserve it, when it is in your power to act" (3:27). Evil is quite another matter. Do good as enabled to do so. Otherwise, one may compound the problem he or she seeks to resolve.

"Do not say to your neighbor, 'Come back later; I'll give it tomorrow'—when you now have it with you." The need may be more pressing. Even if not, delay leads to uncertainty. Procrastination can also be habit forming.

---

1. Inch, *Understanding Bible Prophecy,* 70.

Prudence

"Do not plot harm against your neighbor, who lives trustfully near you." Here the focus shifts from sins of omission to commission. Trust is meant to be rewarded. And it is exceedingly difficult to restore.

"Do not accuse a man for no reason—when he has done no harm." As those who delight in seeing others afflicted. Or some who feel driven to manipulate others in seeking their own advantage.

Although caution is advocated above, it is not to the exclusion of forthright action. Sometimes the worst thing to do is to do nothing. In such instances it does not qualify as prudent.

In addition, one should not approach his or her tasks indifferently. "Whatever you do, work at it with all your heart, as working for the Lord, not for men, since you know that you will receive an inheritance from the Lord as a reward" (Col. 3:23). Having been freed from the drudgery of routine duties, those in Christ find it prudent to fulfill their tasks faithfully.

Conscience coaches prudence in how one ought to behave. Sometimes it cautions against unwise action, and on other occasions it suggests a wise alternative. In this regard, "Dishonest money dwindles away, but he who gathers money little by little makes it grow" (Prov. 13:11).

"Where conscience is crippled or stunted, prudence is also impotent and uncertain. A conscience that is sound, alert, forthright is the best guarantee for the correctness of the prudential acts of deliberation and judgment."[2] Conscience can be readily compromised by personal indiscretion or cultural mores. As for the former, Samson procured the services of a prostitute (cf. Judg. 16:1). It appears in context that he suffered from unbridled passion.

As concerns cultural practices, one is reminded of child sacrifice. So it was that the Lord meant to test Abraham's fidelity: "Take your son, your only son, Isaac, whom you love, and go to the region of Moriah. Sacrifice him there as a burnt offering on one of the mountains I will tell you about" (Gen. 22:2). Then, when he was about to do so, the angel of the Lord protested: "Do not lay

---

2. Haring, *op. cit.*, vol. 1, 506.

a hand on the boy"—since such culturally approved practice was manifestly unacceptable.

Memory also plays a critical role in prudence. Thus past experience is continually being refined to guide contemporary behavior. The memory pattern is to some degree shared with others. Initially, in that we are all human. What we share in common is more substantial than in the many ways we differ.

"When I consider your heavens, the work of your fingers, the moon and the stars, which you have put in place," the psalmist rhetorically inquires, "what is man that you are mindful of him, the son of man that you care for him?" You made him a little lower than the heavenly beings, and crowned him with glory and honor" (8:3–5). Whereupon, he is unique among God's creatures, meant to act as a steward of creation.

Secondly, certain memory patterns are derived from one's ethnic origins. This is more pronounced in some instances than others. For instance, it can be readily com-promised in cross-cultural situations.

This reminds me of the time one of my Nigerian students observed, "When I think of you, it is not as if you were an American but a Nigerian." It seemed to him that I had taken on some of the cultural pattern of his people. As a result, he felt more at ease in my company.

Thirdly, there are more regional adaptations. A certain syndicated columnist period-ically refers to himself as a *southerner*. While of Jewish extraction, he senses much in common with other persons raised in his area of the country. In particular, he seems to cherish the civility cultivated in his cultural context.

Of course, these cultural features are viewed to some degree from different per-spectives. Whether, for instance, from the viewpoint of Euro-American or Afro-American. These, in turn, differ from their overseas counterparts.

Finally, an individual's memory pattern is distinctive. This is true even when raised in the same family, as were my brother and I. Not only did we have different experiences, but we responded differently. For instance, he would characteristically curl up in a chair to read, while I rushed off to shoot baskets.

In traditional societies, one's name was employed as a means of identification. As such, it might be derived from some respected member of the family, in the hope that he or she will emulate the other's precedent. Or it might recall some experience, and thus act as a link to the past. Consequently, it bears repeating that memory solicits prudent be-havior.

Prudence also calls for critical insight. "You give a tenth of your spices—mint, dill and cummin," Jesus protested—as touched on previously. "But you have neglected the more important matters of the law—justice, mercy and faithfulness. You should have practiced the latter, without neglecting the former. You blind guides! You strain out a gnat but swallow a camel" (Matt. 23:23–24).

"Although these verses explicitly criticize the Pharisees' practice, we are surely justified, in view of the context, in seeing here an implicit attack on their teaching. It is assumed that they teach others to imitate their careful tithing of garden herbs and thus draw attention away from God's *moral* will."[3] In particular, their reasoning appears to have been that if one is faithful in lesser matters, he or she is more likely to be faithful in more substantial matters. This, however, appears to be no guarantee.

Conversely, the triad of *justice*, *mercy*, and *faithfulness* brings to bear moral concerns of major consequence. As for *justice*, we have considered this at some length as the first of the cardinal virtues. As such, it was thought necessary in cultivating a moral society.

As for *mercy*, it implies compassion resulting in leniency and forgiveness. In this connection, "the kingdom of heaven is like a king who wanted to settle accounts with his servants. As he began the settlement, a man who owed him ten thousand talents was brought to him. Since he was not able to pay, the master ordered that he and his wife and his children and all that he had be sold to repay the debt" (Matt. 18:23–25).

At this, the servant pled: "Be patient with me, and I will pay back everything." So it was that his master took pity on him, and

---

3. Hare, *op. cit.*, 269.

let him go. Upon leaving, he encountered a fellow servant—who owed him a small sum. "Pay me back what you owe me!" he demanded.

"Be patient with me, and I will pay you back," his fellow servant petitioned. However, he refused and had the fellow thrown into prison.

When this was brought to the attention of his master, the latter rebuked him: "You wicked servant, I canceled all that debt of yours because you begged me to. Shouldn't you have had mercy on your fellow servant just as I had on you?" He then in anger had the servant turned over to the jailors to be abused until he paid back what was owed.

"This is how my heavenly Father will treat each of you unless you forgive your brother from your heart," Jesus pointedly concluded. Unless they showed mercy, result-ing in forgiveness.

As for *faithfulness*, this suggests a dutiful response. Accordingly, the psalmist declares: "I have chosen the way of truth; I have set my heart on your love. I hold fast to your statues, O Lord; do not let me be put to shame. I run in the path of your commands, for you have set my heart free" (119:30–32).

"The word of God calls for both obedience and faith. The right hearing is a faith that obeys and an obedience that believes, both together, as if one response. To hear is to choose the way of faithfulness."[4] Accordingly, to *hear* is to *heed*. We are thus assured that prudence involves more than simply expediency, but draws on negotiating life with respect to divine guidance.

"Insight needs to be combined with reasoned application. That is, it is necessary to address the issue at hand. Otherwise, one will most likely have to settle for some moral platitude."[5] In other words, one must take care to establish a plausible connection between moral ideals and the given context.

"Suppose a brother or sister is without clothes and daily food," James raises a hypothetical issue. "If one of you says to him, 'Go, I wish you well; keep warm and well fed,' but does nothing about

4. Mays, *Psalms*, 385.
5. Inch, *Why Take the Bible Seriously?*, 52.

his physical needs, what good is it? In the same way, faith by itself, if it is not accompanied by actions, is dead" (2:15-17). Prudence requires that we do not simply wish people well, but attempt to meet their needs.

As noted in passing, there exists a hierarchy of needs. These begin with such as are necessary for survival: food, housing, clothing, and health. They extend to matters related to security, esteem, and fulfillment. Prudent behavior characteristically becomes more complex as one ascends the hierarchy of needs.

One thing further. Prudence is fostered by humility. This should not be confused with self-depreciation, which like pride is unduly concerned with self. Which gives rise to the cynical remark, "I am humble, and proud of it."

Humility, conversely, is not reluctant to admit our faults, and make amends when possible. "Lord, Lord!" Zacchaeus exclaimed. "Here and now I give a half of my possessions to the poor, and if I have cheated anybody out of anything, I will pay back four times the amount" (Luke 19:8).

Whereupon, Jesus commended him: "Today salvation has come to this house." As a result of his prudent behavior.

Initially, the proverbs are introduced "for giving prudence to the simple" (Prov. 1:4). In context, prudence is associated with *discipline, understanding, proverbs, sayings*, and *riddles*. Which recalls the saying, "one is known by the company he (in this instance, *it*) keeps."

"A fool shows his annoyance at once, but a prudent man overlooks an insult" (12:16). In greater detail, a *fool* resists instruction; otherwise expressed, he is obstinate; as the saying goes, he "resembles an accident waiting to happen;" and as such is a menace to him or herself and others. Consequently, "The contrast is between mindless and spontaneous reaction of anger and a calm, deliberate response."[6] Self-control is a common prudential theme in wisdom literature.

"A prudent man keeps his knowledge to himself, but the heart of fools blurts out folly" (v. 23). As for the former, he or she shows discretion by choosing the appropriate time and means of

---

6. Murphy and Hunter, *Proverbs, Ecclesiastes, Song of Songs*, 60.

expressing oneself. As for the latter, the person simply blurts out his or her opinion—without due consideration for its consequences.

"Every prudent man acts out of knowledge, but a fool exposes his folly" (13:16). The former is thus guided by reliable instruction, while the latter reveals his lack thereof. Qualifications aside, these contrasting responses come about as a natural consequence of their respective inner dispositions.

Of similar intent, "The wisdom of the prudent is to give thought to their ways, but the folly of fools is deception" (14:8). Whereas the prudent see their way clearly, the foolish deceive themselves. And in deceiving themselves, they may well deceive others.

"A simple man believes anything, but a prudent man gives thought to his steps" (v. 15). The *simple* may be uninformed, or if not, have not committed themselves to some course of action. Conversely, a prudent person carefully considers the alternatives, and chooses among them.

"The simple inherit folly, but the prudent are crowned with knowledge" (v. 18). The former acquire folly as a result of not attending to instruction, while the latter are rewarded with knowledge. Then, with knowledge, they can cultivate skill in negotiating life. As applicable to this situation, "For everyone who has will be given more, and he will have an abundance. Whoever does not have, even what he has will be taken from him" (Matt. 25:28-29).

"Houses and wealth are inherited from parents, but a prudent wife is from the Lord" (19:14). While all things were thought to be under divine supervision, some involved human factors more than others. "Among these were inheritance laws that could ensure a more or less mechanical transfer. One need only be born in a family of some means. However, certain moves in life were beyond human control. Therefore a truly good *wife* had to be seen as a (mysterious) gift from God (cf. 18:22; 31:10-31)."[7] Consequently, prudence itself might be construed as a divine gift, one to be cherished and enhanced.

---

7. Ibid., 85.

11

Temperance

TEMPERANCE WOULD QUALIFY AS a prime example of prudent behavior. As such, it appeals for moderation in action, thought, and/or feeling. According to the sage, "There can be too much of a good thing." Such as is the case with gluttony.

As for the latter, "Do not join those who drink too much wine or gorge themselves on meat, for drunkards and gluttons become poor, and drowsiness clothes them in rags" (Prov. 23:20–21). This caution is expressed in social terms, since one is readily enticed by others to participate in unsuitable practice. Drunkenness and eating in excess are strictly forbidden.

Wine served a variety of purposes in antiquity. For instance, we read that the good Samaritan bandaged the wounds of the man fallen prey to robbers, *pouring on oil and wine* (cf. Luke 10:34). In this instance, it served as a disinfectant. Whereas the oil was meant to enhance the healing process.

Another example enjoins, "Give wine to those who are in anguish; let them drink and forget their poverty and remember their misery no more" (Prov. 31:6–7). Wine is thus cast in the role as a pain reliever. This appears with reference to persons who are passing away. If so, more effective means have been found to ease their pain. This also recalls stories concerning persons who were operated on without any anesthesia other than strong drink.-

Wine was also employed as a means of neutralizing the high alkaline content in water. This is likely the context for Paul's admonition to Timothy, "Stop drinking only water, and use a little wine because of your stomach and your frequent illnesses" (1 Tim. 5:23).

"It is agreeable, therefore, to right reason, to drink on account of the cold of winter, till the numbness is dispelled from those who are subject to feel it," Clement of Alexandria speculates further; "and on occasions as a medicine for the intestines. For, as we are to use food to satisfy hunger, so also are we to use drink to satisfy thirst, taking the most careful precautions against a slip: 'For the introduction of wine is perilous.'"[1]

He compares drunkenness "to the danger of the sea, in which when the body has once been sunken like a ship, it descends into the turpitude, and the helmsman, the human mind, is tossed about and buried in the trough of the sea, is blinded by the darkness of the tempest, having drifted away from the haven of truth, till, dashing on the rocks beneath the sea, it perishes." Whether in this regard or some other, such as those lacking in temperance.

Furthermore, it was common practice in antiquity to dilute the mixture of wine and water. For instance, the rabbis taught that unless wine was diluted, it could not be blessed. Some required three parts water, six, or even more before declaring it acceptable. Accordingly, wisdom personified "has prepared her meat and mixed her wine; she has also set her table. She has sent out her maids, and she calls from the highest point of the city, 'Let all who are simple come in here! Come, eat my food and drink the wine I have mixed'" (Prov. 9:5).

In contrast, the personification of folly tempts those who pass her way: "'Stolen water is sweet, food eaten in secret is delicious!' But little do they know that the dead are there" (vv. 17–18). Thus the reoccurring imagery of the two ways (cf. Psa. 1) are set over against one another, as concerns the way of righteousness eventuating in life, and wick-edness terminating in death.

1. Clement of Alexandria, *The Instructor*, II, 2.

Temperance

Persons are especially admonished not to drink wine when it may impair their ability to carry out some duty assigned to them. For instance, "It is not for kings to drink wine, lest they drink and forget what the law decrees, and deprive all the oppressed of their rights" (Prov. 31:4-5). Which may mean that they should refrain when acting in their official capacity.

This also brings to mind the Nazarite vow. In particular, "If a man or woman wants to make a special vow, a vow of separation to the Lord as a Nazarite, he must abstain from wine and other fermented drink. (Num. 6:2-3). "The prohibition could be a protest against the lifestyle of intoxication, decadence, or degeneracy, or an avoidance of what is fermented. Fermentation causes a change in the liquid that blurs the classification of the substances and so violates the Priestly categories of creation."[2]

The second part of the vow prohibits the cutting of one's hair (cf. vv. 5-8). While the symbolism is obscure, commentators as a rule attribute it to the vitality of life, and hence God—as the Giver of life. If something more, it was perhaps thought to be a sign of wisdom—cultivated by the Lord God.

This general line of reasoning has expanded application today. Driving under the influence of intoxicating drink naturally comes to mind in this connection. Not simply when in access of that which is allowed, but so as to otherwise impair one's ability.

In like manner, the practice of employing a cell phone while driving should be discouraged—based on the same premise. Consequently, it is subject to the virtue of temperance. In this and other ways, the appeal to temperance seems timely.

Gluttony is prohibited along with drunkenness. "Do not join those who drink too much wine or gorge themselves on meat," the sage enjoins, "for drunkards and gluttons become poor, and drowsiness clothes them in rags" (Prov. 23:20-21). In more graphic terms, this constitutes the road from revelry to rags.

In any case, some people will find cause for complaint. "For John came neither eating nor drinking, and they say, 'He has a demon,'" Jesus observed. "The Son of Man came eating and drinking,

---

2. Bellinger, Jr., *Leviticus, Numbers*, 200.

and they say, 'Here is a glutton and a drunkard, a friend of tax collectors and 'sinners''' (Matt. 11:18–19).

Instead, they meticulously fostered a pseudo-temperance in the form of a stifling legalism. Whereas, its genuine counterpart allows for a range of responses, dictated in some measure by circumstances. This recalls the pertinent observation: "There is a time for everything, and a season for every activity under heaven" (Eccles. 3:1). By way of illustration, "a time to weep and a time to laugh, a time to search and a time to give up, a time to be silent and a time to speak."

"In the poem, pairs of opposites illustrate that there is a proper time for all human activity. When it is read in isolation from its context, the poem provides the reader with a sense of comfort and assurance."[3] Consequently, it serves as a deterrent against intemperate behavior.

It could also be pointed out, "There is a time to exercise and a time to refrain." "For physical training is of some value," Paul allows, "but godliness has value for all things, holding promise for both the present life and the life to come" (1 Tim. 4:8). Physical training is valuable if not overdone. Otherwise, health is impaired.

The issue is compounded when one suffers an injury. I speak from experience, recalling occasions when I had to weigh whether to play or wait until more fully recovered. On the one hand, temperance does not dictate that we should pamper ourselves. On the other, it restrains us from disregarding sage advice.

In contrast, the apostle points out that *godliness* profits without qualification, *holding promise* both for the present and the future. Accordingly, it serves as an encouragement to exercise temperance—along with the other cardinal virtues. Which recalls the sage saying, "The more some things change, the more other matters appear constant."

We are also alerted to the fact, "There is a time to sleep, and a time to arise." In this regard, "He who gathers crops in summer is a wise son, but he who sleeps during harvest is a disgraceful

---

3. Murphy and Hunter, *op. cit.*, 187.

son" (Prov. 19:5). When pressing duties await, this is not a time to procrastinate by excessive rest.

Conversely, some fail to get proper relaxation. Instead, they drive themselves relent-lessly. This proves to be counter-productive. Lacking in moderation, they are prone to become ill-tempered and troublesome.

In addition, there is an occasion to commend, and a time to withhold commendation. Such as we are experiencing in our educational system, where increasing numbers of our high school graduates are unable to pass basic tests in core subjects. This problem is compounded by the effort to enhance self-esteem, and the lowering of standards to accommodate.

On the other hand, incentives are as a rule more effective than disapproval. Or as C. S. Lewis graphically expresses the options, God is more inclined to employ *carrots* than *clubs*. Even when it is difficult to give blanket approval, it is important to single out some feature as praiseworthy.

Furthermore, "There is a time to live and a time to die." This being the case, one is not ready to live until he or she has come to grips with death. This serves as a needed reality check to put other matters in proper focus.

Conversely, one is not ready to die until he or she has been involved in living. From a Christian perspective, the afterlife is an extension of our present existence. Whether for better or worse, we sow what we reap—temperance being one of our most useful means of negotiating the exigencies of life.

At this juncture, we return to the early church fathers for further input. Tertullian addressed the topic of modesty, which is yet another feature of temperance. "Modesty, the flower of manners, the honor of our bodies, the grace of the sexes, the integrity of the blood, the guarantee of our race, the basis of sanctity, the pre-indication of every good disposition; rare though it is" still survives our degradation.[4]

He begins with the prohibition against sexual immorality, resulting from incest, and solicited by immodesty. As for sexual

---

4. Tertullian, *On Modesty*, I

immorality, he defers to the decision of the Jerusalem Council: "You are to abstain from food sacrificed to idols, from blood, from the meat of strangled animals and from sexual immorality" (Acts 15:29). As noted in an earlier context, *sexual immorality* is apparently used in comprehensive fashion to pre-clude any deviant sexual practice.

As for incest, Clement of Alexandria observes: "But by no manner of means are women to be allowed to uncover and exhibit any part of their person, lest both fall,—the men by being excited to look, they by drawing on themselves the eyes of the men. But always must we conduct ourselves as in the Lord's presence."[5]

As for modesty, "Follow God, stripped of arrogance, stripped of fading display, possessed of that which is thine, which is good, what alone cannot be taken away—faith towards God, confession towards Him who suffered, beneficence towards men, which is the most precious of possessions."[6] Instead of focusing on those things which are superficial, transitory, and demeaning.

"Give me neither poverty nor riches, but give me only my daily bread," the sage petitions. "Otherwise, I may have too much and disown you and say, 'Who is the Lord?' Or I may become poor and steal, and so dishonor the name of my God" (Prov. 30:8-9). If poverty stricken, then tempted to steal. If affluent, then self-sufficient. If neither, then amenable to the virtue of temperance.

"Temperance requires discipline. Whereas eating does not require discipline, eating in moderation does. Whereas sex does not require discipline, responsible sex does. And so it goes, from one aspect of life to another."[7] Discipline thus extends not simply to the quantity of food one eats, but its selection. Accordingly, mother would insist that something was good for me, although not necessarily appealing.

Similarly, discipline involves not only the frequency with which we engage in sex, but with whom we do so. This recalls the sordid story of Lot's two daughters, who got their father drunk in

---

5. Clement of Alexandria, *The Instructor*, II, 2.
6. Ibid., II, 3.
7. Inch, *Why Take the Bible Seriously?*, 53.

order to have sex with him. "So both of Lot's daughters became pregnant by their father" (Gen. 19:36). And so it bears repeating, *temperance requires discipline.*

Temperance must also be deliberately acquired. First in one context, and then another. Drawing upon credible mentors, while assuming responsibility as capable of doing so. Not distracted by extraneous matters, while bent on receiving the commendation: "Well done, good and faithful servant! You have been faithful with a few things; I will put you in charge of many things" (Matt. 25:21).

Temperance likewise requires persistent resolve. It is tempting to slack off, especially when the task seems overwhelming. "Not that I have already obtained all this, or have already been made perfect," Paul allows, "but I press on to take hold of that for which Christ Jesus took hold of me" (Phil. 12).

"But one thing I do," he continues: "Forgetting what is behind and straining toward what is ahead, I press on toward the goal to win the prize for which God has called me heavenward in Christ Jesus." Thus recalling our earlier consideration of *in Christ* as instrumental in Christian ethics.

"Enter through the narrow gate," Jesus enjoined his listeners. "For wide is the gate and broad is the road that leads to destruction, and many enter through it. But small is the gate and narrow the road that leads to life, and only a few find it" (Matt. 7:13-14). Such would seem to be confirmed by our brief excursion into the virtue of temperance, and especially given its notable lack.

12

Fortitude

FORTITUDE ROUNDS OUT THE list of cardinal virtues. "It is the role of this virtue to repress the rebellion of the emotions against suffering and death, to discipline and control all the deep sentiments of fear and terror, if they should attempt to interfere with our generous engagement of the good, even at the cost of life itself."[1] It is fortitude that cultivates moral resolve in the face of discouragement, opposition, and weariness.

Fortitude thus comprises both negative and positive features. As for the former, one must resist those inclinations which would subvert moral endeavor. "Watch and pray so that you do not fall into temptation," Jesus enjoined Peter. "The spirit is willing, but the body is weak" (Matt. 26:41). "Human nature cannot always measure up to the noble aspirations of the spirit. In the most central conflict of human existence Jesus exhibited the victory of the spirit over the flesh while the disciples displayed the victory of the flesh over the spirit."[2]

The admonition to *watch* implies discernment. One must learn to distinguish be-tween that which is morally accountable and repugnant. This is not necessarily evident, even for those with

---

1. Haring, *op. cit.*, vol. 1, 525.
2. Mounce, *op. cit.*, 244.

Fortitude

good intentions. Hence, the admonition to *pray* for guidance and enablement is especially appropriate.

"When tempted, no one should say, 'God is tempting me.' For God cannot be tempted by evil, nor does he tempt anyone; but each one is tempted when, by his own evil desire, he is dragged away and enticed" (James 1:13-14). While God may *test* persons by way of confirming and fortifying their faith, he does not try to lead them astray. It remains that humans should not welcome temptation, but steadfastly resist it. And here fortitude comes into play.

Not only refrain from doing evil, but do good. "Put on the full armor of God so that you can take your stand against the devil's schemes. For our struggle is not against flesh and blood, but against the rulers, against the authorities, against the powers of this dark world and against the spiritual forces of evil in the heavenly realms" (Eph. 6:11-12).

Since the enemy is powerful, wicked, and shrewd, it must not be taken lightly. "Stand firm then, with the belt of truth buckled around your waist, with the breastplate of righteousness in place, and with your feet fitted with the readiness that comes from the gospel of peace." In addition, "take the shield of faith, with which you can extinguish all the flaming arrows of the evil one. Take the helmet of salvation and the sword of the Spirit, which is the word of God." Pray also without ceasing.

"Do not be deceived: God cannot be mocked. A man reaps what he sows. The one who sows to please his sinful nature, will reap destruction; the one who sows to please the Spirit, from the Spirit will reap eternal life" (Gal. 6:7-8). Consequently, "Let us not become weary in doing good, for at the proper time we will reap a harvest if we do not give up. Therefore, as we have opportunity, let us do good to all people, especially to those who belong to the family of believers."

At a proper time serves as an encouragement in anticipation of what will transpire. It also cautions those who fail to take the exhortation seriously. While obligated to do good to all persons, the *family of believers* solicits special attention—given a common bond in Christ. Thus the virtue of fortitude plays out in context of the apostle's deliberation.

Fortitude must likewise contend with both rational and irrational fear. In this regard, "For I fear the slander of many; there is terror on every side; they conspire against me and plot to take my life" (Psa. 31:13). Whereas the Psalmist earlier expresses his trust in the Lord, here fear rises to the surface. One is thus alerted to life's uncertainty and vulnerability.

His fears were associated with a fragile social structure. *Many* persons slandered him, perhaps falsifying the situation or portraying it in an unfavorable light. It appears as if there was a chorus of dissent. Whether an accurate assessment or not, this was legitimate cause to incite fear.

Terror confronted him *on every side*. There seems to be no exception. This would apparently include both perceived friends and foes alike. In contrast, "A friend loves at all times, and a brother is born for adversity" (Prov. 17:17).

These threatening individuals *conspire* against him. Thus to harm him, in whatever form this might take. Perhaps through the seizure of his property, and/or with physical harm. There are numerous possibilities, each adding to the sense of dread.

This culminates with the *plot to take my life*. While it may appear to be a worst-case scenario, it is not always the case. For instance, in a shame-oriented culture, death might be preferred to shame. "Let love and faithfulness never leave you; bind them around your neck, write them on the tablet of your heart," the sage admonishes. "Then you will win favor and a good name in the sight of God and man" (Prov. 3:3–4).

Having weathered the storm, the psalmist piously reflects: "In my alarm I said, 'I am cut off from your sight!' Yet you heard my cry for mercy when I called to you for help" (v. 22).

"If an enemy were insulting me, I could endure it; if a foe were raising himself against me, I could hide from him. But it is you, a man like myself, my companion, my close friend, with whom I once enjoyed sweet fellowship as we walked with the throng at the

Fortitude

house of God" (Psa. 55:12–14). More threatening is the abuse of a friend than that of a sworn enemy.

Thoughts of the past trouble him. If a supposed friend could turn against him, wherein lies one's confidence? He is driven to unrelenting prayer (cf. v. 17). In this connection, he is assured that the Lord will not forsake him.

He perhaps fears lest he himself will follow suit. In doing so, he will leave the congregation of the righteous, and join with the wicked. The fear of failure grips him, and will not let go.

"Cast your cares on the Lord and he will sustain you," he assures those who must contend with similar uncertainties. "But as for me, I trust in you (the Living Lord)." In terms of the gospel lyrics, "The God on the mountain is the God in the valley."

"Have no fear of sudden disaster or of the ruin that overtakes the wicked," the sage admonishes, "for the Lord will be your confidence and will keep your foot from being snared" (Prov. 3:25–26). Unexpected disaster can be especially threatening. It may occur when we least expect it, along with disastrous results. We lack the time seemingly necessary to cope with it.

The tragic results *that overtake the wicked* can intensify the problem. They increase their vulnerability by their wicked behavior. Conversely, the godly prove not to be im-mune from adversity.

One document lists over 1000 objects that incite fear. For instance, there is *acro-phobia*—fear of heights, *xenophobia*—fear of new ideas, *decidophia*—fear of having to make decisions, *heterophobia*—fear of the opposite sex, and *sociophobia*—fear of social gatherings. In a more humorous vein, there is *arachbutyrophobia*—fear of peanut butter sticking to the roof of one's mouth. Fear can thus be said to range from the profound to the trivial.

Having considered the need for fortitude to manage fear, we turn to suffering as graphically set forth in the Job narrative. Job was a strikingly devout person, beset by adversity. He was stripped of his wealth, family, and health. The cosmic struggle between good and evil played out in the background.

Three friends try to console him in his suffering. However, each has a personal agenda. Subsequently, a fourth joins them, but adds little of constructive value. "Even-tually the Lord Himself addresses Job. These speeches change Job's attitude, for he responds with contrite submission. In the end God declares Job to be in the right and restores his prosperity and happiness."[3]

In greater detail, "In the land of Uz there lived a man whose name was Job. This man was blameless and upright; he feared God and shunned evil" (Job 1:1). His demeanor greatly pleased the Almighty.

It came to pass that the angels came to present themselves before the Lord God, and Satan was among them. "Have you considered my servant Job?" the Lord inquired of him. "There is no one on earth like him; he is blameless and upright, a man who fears God and shuns evil."

"Does Job fear God for nothing!" the adversary protested. "Have you not put a hedge around him and his household and everything he has?" Here we are subtlety alerted to the fact that righteousness commonly cultivates health and results in an increase of material possessions.

"Very well, then," the Lord allowed, "everything he has is in your hands, but on the man himself do not lay a finger." There follows a series of calamities in rapid succession. At this, the patriarch struggled to his feet, tore his clothes, and shaved his head—as a sign of mourning. Then prostrating himself, he observed: "Naked I came from my mother's womb, and naked I will depart. The Lord gave and the Lord has taken away; may the name of the Lord be praised" (v. 21). "In all this," the chronicler appreciatively observes, "Job did not sin by charging God with wrongdoing." Fortitude having come to his rescue.

Another day the angels came to present themselves before the Lord, and Satan was again with them. "Have you considered my servant Job?" the Lord again inquires. "There is no one on earth like him, he is blameless and upright, a man who fears God and shuns evil. And he still maintains his integrity, although you incited me against him to ruin him without any reason" (2:3).

"Skin for skin!" Satan exclaims. "A man will give all he has for his own life. But stretch out your hand and strike his flesh and

---

3. Andersen, *Job*, 15.

bones, and he will surely curse you to your face." He seems determined to undermine the patriarch's integrity.

"Very well, then," the Lord allowed, "he is in your hands, but you must spare his life." "So it was that the adversary afflicted Job with painful sores from the sole of his feet to the top of his head. Then the patriarch took a piece of broken pottery, and scraped himself with it as he sat among the ashes. The reference is likely to the rubbish dump outside the city, perhaps indicating that he was an outcast."[4]

"Are you still holding to your integrity?" his wife incredulously inquired. "Curse God and die!" This appears preferable to prolonged suffering.

"You are talking like a foolish woman," Job protests. "Shall we accept good from God, and not trouble?" "In all this," the chronicler again observes, "Job did not sin in what he said." He was thus commended for his manifest fortitude.

Fortitude also assists us in negotiating death, as we are reminded by the Christian martyrs. Stephen first invites our attention. At a time when the numbers of disciples were rapidly increasing, there arose a problem concerning the distribution of food. In particular, the *Grecian Jews* complained that their widows were being overlooked.

"The Hellenists of this passage were Christians drawn from the Greek-speaking synagogues of Jerusalem, and forming their own Greek-speaking community. The apostles themselves were, of course, Hebrews."[5] Consequently, the neglect appears to have been unintentional.

Since the apostles were engaged in other demanding activities, it was decided to select others to assume oversight. Stephen was one of those chosen. As such, he was characterized as being *full of the Spirit and wisdom*. This was borne out in his success in defending the claims of Christ against belligerent opposition.

He was, nonetheless, brought before the Sanhedrin (cf. Acts 6:8–14). There he bore witness to his faith. At this, the people

---

4. Inch, *Pain As a Means of Grace*, 16–17.
5. Williams, *Acts*, 118.

covered their ears and shouting at the top of their voices, dragged him out of the city and began to stone him. While being stoned, he prayed: "Lord Jesus, receive my spirit." Then he fell on his knees and cried out: "Lord, do not hold this sin against them." He thus conveyed a peaceful submission, and forgiving spirit. Saul (Paul) approvingly observed what transpired, which likely left a lasting impression on him.

Ignatius serves as another case in point. "When Trojan, not long since, succeeded to the empire of the Romans (AD 98), Ignatius, the disciple of John the apostle, governed the Church of the Antiochians with great care, having with difficulty escaped the former storms of the many persecutions under Domitian."[6] He composed seven extant epistles while in transit from Antioch to Rome, where he would suffer martyrdom.

"For even though I am in bonds for his Name's sake," Ignatius allows, "I am not yet perfected in Jesus Christ."[7] He thus portrays himself as a work in progress. "Once associated with the ministry at Antioch, now concerning his incarceration, and eventually with his martyrdom. Each succeeding stage is calculated to prepare him for the one to follow."[8]

"It is good for me to die for Jesus Christ rather than to reign over the farthest bounds of the earth," he declares.[9] "What is more," Paul writes in this connection, "I consider everything loss compared to the surpassing greatness of knowing Christ Jesus my Lord, for whose sake I have lost all things. I consider them rubbish, that I may gain Christ and be found in him" (Phil. 3:8).

Everything allows for no exceptions. Not the prospect of dominion, nor of popular acclaim; not a long life, nor good health. Accordingly, Ignatius urges that his fellow believers not attempt to circumvent his impending martyrdom. Since he considers it the final stage in his sanctification and ministry

---

6. *The Martyrdom of Ignatius*, I.
7. Ignatius, *To the Ephesians*, 3.
8. Inch, *Pain As a Means of Grace*, 4.
9. Ignatius, *To the Romans*, 6.

IV

Theological Virtues

13

Faith

WE TURN OUR ATTENTION from cardinal to theological virtues, the latter being more explicitly associated with salvation history. Accordingly, they are likewise related to being *in Christ*. In particular, they consist of faith, hope, and love. "And now these three remain," Paul assures us: "faith, hope and love. But the greatest of these is love" (1 Cor. 13:13).

"Together these words embrace the whole of Christian existence, as believers live out the life of the Spirit in the present age, awaiting the consummation. They have 'faith' toward God, that is, they trust him to forgive and accept them through Christ."[1] In addition, they "have 'hope' for the future, which has been guaranteed them through Christ." Furthermore, "they have 'love' for one another as they live this life of faith and hope in the context of a community of brothers and sisters of similar faith and hope." *Love* is singled out since it remains applicable, even after *faith* and *hope* have served their purposes.

Faith, nonetheless, first solicits our consideration. In this connection, we turn to the famous chapter concerning faith (cf. Heb. 11). "The author's purpose in this magnificent section of his letter

---

1. Fee, *The First Epistle to the Corinthians*, 650.

is to encourage his readers to emulate these heroes and heroines of faith, who on the basis of what they knew about God and his promises had the courage to move out into the unknown, with their hearts set upon, and their lives controlled by, a great unseen reality."[2]

"Now faith is being sure of what we hope for and certain of what we do not see. This is what the ancients were commended for" (v. 1–2). The text allows for both an objective and subjective application. As for the former, faith embraces God's promises. As for the latter, it consists of implicit trust.

"By faith we understand that the universe was formed of God's command, so that what is seen was not made out of what was visible" (v. 3). Creation thus provides a model for faith, since that which we see came into being by way of that which we do not see. This was in response to God's *word*, and hence expressive of his power.

In greater detail, "By faith Abel offered God a better sacrifice than Cain did. By faith he was commended as a righteous man, when God spoke well of his offering. And for faith he still speaks, even though he is dead" (v. 4). As touched on earlier, Abel offered *a better sacrifice* since it consisted of a choice portion, whereas Cain's offering was of perfunctory nature.

Whereupon, he was commended *as a righteous man*. That is, one who lives in accordance with God's gracious will. He thus becomes open to divine initiatives, and available to minister to others. This is on the basis of his confidence in an unseen reality, and results as yet to be realized.

Even though dead, he still speaks to us concerning faith. While circumstances differ considerably, *faith* remains essentially the same. Thus according to the sage, "Should we fail to learn from the past, we are destined to repeat its faults."

"By faith Enoch was taken from this life, so that he did not experience death; he could not be found, because God had taken him away. For before he was taken, he was commended as one who pleased God" (v. 5). The author does not dwell on his ascension, except as it confirmed Enoch *as one who pleased God*.

2. Hagner, *Hebrews*, 179.

Faith and *obedience* thus come into play. In brief, those who believe, obey; and those who obey, believe. This rejects a dichotomy between faith and works, opting in-stead for a faith that works.

"And without faith it is impossible to please God," the author adds, "because anyone who comes to him must believe that he exists and that he rewards those who earnestly seek him" (v. 6). He *exists* in contrast to the myriad of false deities proposed, bearing in mind that the rabbis reasoned that idolatry was the ultimate source of evil. Likewise, considering the fact that it is not always the flagrant evil we do but the lesser good that frustrates God's purposes.

Not only does he exist, but *he rewards those who diligently seek him*. His *rewards* consist of unimaginable spiritual blessings, for which our present experience provides an earnest. These are reserved for those who *diligently seek him*, in persistent fashion and not distracted by other considerations.

"By faith Noah, when warned about things not seen, in holy fear built an ark to save his family. By his faith he condemned the world and became heir of the righteousness that comes by faith" (v. 7). *Things not seen* implicitly implies both promise and caution. Consequently, the *righteousness that comes by faith* amounts to acting in accord with the anticipated results.

"For whence was Noah 'found righteous,' if in his case the righteousness of a natural law had not preceded?" Tertullian rhetorically inquires.[3] This was by way of pointing out that morality did not originate with the Mosaic Covenant, but is an aspect of life as we experience it. Accordingly, it again bears repeating that life ideally resembles a *sacred canopy*.

The roll call of those who exercised faith continues. "By faith Abraham, when called to go to a place he would later receive as his inheritance, obeyed and went, even though he did not know where he was going. By faith he made his home in the promised land like a stranger in a foreign country; he lived in tents, as did Isaac and Jacob, who were heirs with him in the same promise" (vv. 8–9). One does not know what the future holds, but who holds his future.

3. Tertullian, *An Answer to the Jews*, II.

As quoted early on, "They dwell in their own countries, but simply as sojourners. As citizens, they share in all things with others, and yet endure all things as if foreigners. Every foreign land is to them as their native country, and every land of their birth as a land of strangers."[4] For instance, "They marry, as do all; they beget children; but they do not destroy their offspring."

"For he was looking forward to the city with foundations, whose architect and builder is God." So that the Christian life may be described as a journey to the celestial city, as vividly described by John: "It shone with the glory of God, and the brilliance was like that of a very precious jewel, like a jasper, clear as crystal" (Rev. 21:11). Hence, it is inviting and spiritually invigorating.

"By faith Abraham, even though he was past age—and Sarah herself was barren—was enabled to become a father because he considered him faithful who had made the promise. And so from the one man, and he as good as dead, came descendants as numerous as the stars in the sky and as countless as the sand on the seashore" (11–12). The focus here is expressly on Abraham's faith, since his wife was slow to believe.

The patriarch was *as good as dead* insofar as founding a family. We are thus reminded of the exhortation, "Expect great things from God, and undertake great things in his name." Also of Mother Teresa's humorous rejoinder, "I have no doubt that God will enable me to do what he would have me do, but I wish he were not so optimistic."

"All these people were still living by faith when they died. They did not receive the things promised, they only saw them and welcomed them from a distance" (v. 13). *All these people* previously mentioned persisted in their confidence, obstacles notwithstanding. Even when far removed from their fulfillment.

Such is the reliance gained from one generation to the next. As such, it forms a legacy of faith. It is one that can be either ignored or appropriated for the benefit of oneself and others. As for the latter, "God is not ashamed to be called their God" for they demonstrate their confidence in him.

4. *Epistle to Diognetus*, V.

Faith

Having paused to reflect on that which these folk had in common, the author continues with his detailed account. "By faith Abraham . . . who had received the promises was about to sacrifice his one and only son, even though God had said to him, 'It is through Isaac that your offspring will be reckoned.' Abraham reasoned that God could raise the dead, and figuratively speaking, he did receive Isaac back from death" (vv. 17–19).

This constitutes what appears to be the most popular narrative in Jewish devotional literature. Both Abraham and Isaac are portrayed as exemplars of faith. The passage also serves to illustrate various religious and moral considerations; such as faith, devotion, obedience, fidelity, and sacrifice. It should likewise be understood in context where child sacrifice was practiced, but did not receive God's approval.

"By faith Isaac blessed Jacob and Esau in regard to their future" (v. 20). "When he learned that Jacob had received the blessing intended for Esau, he made no attempt to revoke it; rather he confirmed it (cf. Gen. 27:33). Yet he did reserve a blessing for Esau, and although it was not the blessing bound up with the promise, yet it was a blessing concerning 'things to come.'"[5]

Jacob exhibited a vital interest in God's promise apparently not shared by his sibling. Granted, this does not justify his deceit. Once pronounced, it appears that his father felt the blessing was binding.

"By faith Jacob, when he was dying, blessed each of Joseph's sons, and worshiped as he leaned on the top of his staff" (v. 21). He blesses *each of Joseph's sons* as a way of verifying that they are legitimate progenitors of their respective tribes of Israel. Furthermore, the twelve tribes constitute the people of God. As such, they represent a community of faith.

Worship is thus subtly tied to the exercise of faith. Accordingly, we are reminded that the latter honors God and his word. It also recalls the creed's affirmation, "The chief end of man is to glorify God and enjoy him forever."

"By faith Joseph, when his end was near, spoke about the exodus of the Israelites from Egypt and gave instructions about

---

5. Bruce, *The Epistles to the Hebrews*, 305.

his bones" (v. 22). That is, he anticipated that the Israelites would return to the promised land, and requested that his remains accompany them. Even though this event likely did not seem imminent at the time.

As for the destination, "It was a *land between* two great meteorological systems: the dry scorching heat from the desert and the moist breeze from the sea. These struggled to gain and maintain control as if two relentless combatants. This provided the theological imagery for the two ways, concerning the wicked and the righteous."[6]

"By faith Moses' parents hid him for three months after he was born, because they saw he was no ordinary child, and they were not afraid of the king's edict" (v. 23). Faith is thus depicted as embracing others within the scope of God's benevolent design. We thus express confidence in his intent to work on their behalf.

While *no ordinary child* might be simply a reference to his comely appearance, it was perhaps meant to imply some awareness of a special calling. In any case, they were willing to accept the risk of violating the magistrate's prohibition. We are thus reminded that faith can put life in danger.

"By faith Moses, when he had grown up, refused to be known as the son of Pharaoh's daughter. He chose to be mistreated along with the people of God rather than to enjoy the pleasures of sin for a short time" (vv. 24–25). "The fruit of faith has been shown in several ways thus far: for example, confidence concerning the unknown and the future; obedience to the difficult and unexpected command of God; courage in the face of fear. Now the author illustrates how faith enables personal self-denial in the choice of suffering rather than pleasure."[7]

The pleasures of sin are fleeting, while the blessings of God endure. Faith wisely opts for the latter. Better to suffer reproach with the people of God than to enjoy popular acclamation.

"By faith the people passed through the Red Sea as on dry land, but when the Egyptians tried to do so, they were drowned"

6. Inch, *Scripture As Story*, 43.
7. Hagner, *op. cit.*, 200.

(v. 29). Some have speculated that this resulted from volcanic activity in the Aegean Sea. In any case, it was a timely event that honored their corporate faith. So while we are inclined to think of faith in personal terms, it is also something shared with others.

Accordingly, we are reminded of life together. Upon coming to Christ, we find our-selves associated with those of like precious faith. We are aptly enjoined, "Let us not give up meeting together, as some are in the habit of doing, but let us encourage one another—and all the more as you see the Day approaching" (Heb. 10:25).

"By faith the walls of Jericho fell, after the people had marched around them for seven days" (v. 30). Whose faith was implicated? That of Joshua to be sure. That of the people in carrying out his directions. More indirectly, that of those who had primed them to exercise faith.

What material factors were involved in the collapse of Jericho's walls? We cannot be certain. But we are alerted to the fact that it was in answer to intervening faith. This, moreover, is a faith that embraces divine creativity.

"By faith the prostitute Rahab, because she welcomed the spies, was not killed with those who were disobedient" (v. 31). "It is perhaps something of a surprise to find *the prostitute Rahab*, a non-Israelite, mentioned alongside the great names of righteous Israelis. But she too, most remarkably, had come to have faith in the God of Israel, per-haps by hearing of the victories of Israel and the power of Israel's God (cf. Josh. 2:11)."[8]

No less striking is the fact that she was a prostitute. We are thus reminded that Jesus encouraged "sinners" (non-observant Jews) to repent of their sins, and exercise faith in God's forgiveness. Such were often more amenable to his message than those confident in their meticulous religious behavior. Thus faith runs true to course, in spite of some unexpected nuances.

---

8. Ibid., 204.

14

Hope

THOSE LISTED AS EXEMPLARS of faith might as readily qualify as precedents for *hope*. Faith, however, is exercised concerning promise, while hope focuses on fulfillment. As such, they are complimentary. Then, as mentioned earlier, they—along with love—constitute the theological virtues.

The Job narrative again solicits our consideration. Having touched on it earlier, we will focus expressly on texts where hope is acknowledged. This also serves to alert us to the fact that hope provides a prime means for negotiating adversity. While not limited to these instances, it seems to rise to the occasion. If not, despair readily sets in.

"What I feared has come upon me; what I dreaded has happened to me," the patriarch confesses. "I have no rest, but only turmoil" (Job 3:25–26). Contrary to the sage observation, there appears to be no light at the end of the tunnel.

"If someone ventures a word with you, will you be impatient?" Eliphaz inquires. "But who can keep from speaking?" (4:2) It seems that he meant to justify what he was about to say. "Think how you have instructed many, how you have strengthened feeble hands. But now trouble comes to you, and you are discouraged.

Hope

Should not your piety be your confidence and your blameless ways your hope?" (4:3, 6). Demonstrate the same response you have encouraged in others.

Hope in this instance pertains to the confidence that God will reward righteous behavior. "It is one thing to appeal to an abstract principle which seems self-evident to the mind of a man with moral sense. It is quite another to apply it to Job's particular case."[1] Since there is no simple correlation between practice and recompense in this life. So that the wicked not uncommonly prosper, while the upright are afflicted.

Consequently, realistic hope is more in keeping with Paul's assurance: "And we know that in all things God works for the good of those who love him, who have been called according to his purpose" (Rom. 8:28). It certainly does not mean that everything is desirable, which would be inadmissible. Instead, God delights in turning even the worst experience to our advantage. The apostle was speaking from experience.

Eliphaz was of the opinion that Job had grown callous in the midst of riches, and allowed unrighteousness to creep into his life. His adversity served as a warning that he mend his ways. He could repent and be restored to divine favor or persist in his evil ways and suffer the consequences. So the *poor*, those who recognize their need, are candidates for *hope* (cf. 5:16). "Blessed is the m an whom God corrects, so do not despise the discipline of the Almighty" (5:17).

Indeed, we may count on God's forgiveness, if requested and in response to repentance. However, Eliphaz promotes an ancient version of the gospel of prosperity. One that assumes righteousness guarantees riches. In the light of the Job narrative, this appears suspect.

"My days are swifter than a weaver's shuttle, and they come to an end without hope," the patriarch replies (7:6). Life is exceedingly brief, and fraught with difficulties. In particular, "The length of our days is seventy years—or eighty, if we have the strength; yet

---

1. Anderson, op. cit., 112.

their span is but trouble and sorrow, for they quickly pass, and we fly away" (Psa. 90:10).

Accordingly, there is no ultimate hope from a humanistic perspective. Either our hope is in God or it is in vain. It remains to sort out the focus of our assurance.

Bildad subsequently confirms this conclusion, "Such is the destiny of all who forget God, so perishes the hope of the godless" (8:13). In this regard, he appeals to tradition: "Ask the former generations and find out what their fathers learned, for we were born only yesterday and know nothing, and our days on earth are but a shadow" (v. 8).

So it was that C. S. Lewis advocated reading one classic work to balance off each current text we read. Otherwise, we fall prey to cultural myopia. This leads the cynic to observe, "We have forgotten more than we know." If not concerning knowledge, then as pertains to wisdom.

Zophar seems determined to force the patriarch's confession to wrongdoing, as a prelude to restoration. "Surely he recognizes deceitful men," Job is assured (11:11). "Yet if you devote your heart to him and stretch out your hands to him, if you put away the sin that is in your hand, and allow no evil to dwell in your tent, then you will lift up your face without shame; you will stand firm and without fear."

"You will be secure, because there is hope; you will look about you and take your rest in safety" (v. 18). "But the eyes of the wicked will fail, and escape will elude them; their hope will become a dying gasp." While accurate, his appraisal does not weigh the actual circumstances. Conversely, Job reflected a more open attitude, a willingness to examine alternatives, and reappraise previously held opinions. However, he must be presented with compelling evidence.

In brief, he allows for a *reasoned hope*. In particular, one that grapples with the issues and does not project guilt indiscriminately. Hence, one that employs the human prerogative to distinguish between right and wrong.

"At least there is hope for a tree," Job observes. "If it is cut down, it will sprout again, and its new shoots will not fail" (14:7).

Hope

"Thus the body in the sepulcher is like the trees which in winter hide their verdure with deceptive dryness. Why are you in haste for it to revive and return, when the winter is still raw?"[2] It is preferable to await God's wise timing, and escape the complications otherwise implicated.

Minucius Felix reasons further that adversity "is not punishment—it is warfare. For fortitude is strengthened by infirmities, and calamity is very often the discipline of virtue; in addition, strength both of mind and of body grows torpid without the exercise of labor."[3] This recalls the sports saying, "No pain, no gain."

"For what hope has the godless when he is cut off, when God takes away his life?" Job inquires (27:8). He has not learned to call upon the Lord, and is at a loss to rectify his situation. Not so the righteous! "Blessed is the man who does not walk in the counsel of the wicked or stand in the way of sinners or sit in the seat of mockers. But his delight is in the law of the Lord, and on his law he meditates day and night" (Psa. 1:1–2).

"I am angry with you and your two friends, because you have not spoken of me what is right, as my servant Job has," the Lord informed Eliphaz. "My servant Job will pray for you, and I will not deal with you according to your folly" (42:7–8). Thus hope is legitimately extended to the patriarch's insensitive associates.

"The Lord blessed the latter part of Job's life more than the first" (v. 12). His flocks flourished, his family proliferated, and he lived an extended lifetime. For, unlike our culture where old age is often thought of in terms of declining vitality, it was thought an achievement. Thus was his hope vindicated.

Having explored the dynamic of hope in context of the Job narrative, we turn to select texts from the Pauline correspondence. "Therefore, since we have been justified through faith, we have peace with God through our Lord Jesus Christ, through whom we have gained access by faith into this grace in which we now stand," the apostle confidently declares. "And we rejoice in the hope of the glory of God. Not only so, but we also rejoice in our sufferings,

---

2. *The Octavious of Minucius Felix*, XXXIV.
3. Ibid., XXXVI.

because we know that suffering produces perseverance; perseverance, character; and character, hope. And hope does not disappoint us, because God has poured out his love into our hearts by the Holy Sprit, whom he has given us" (Rom. 5:1–5).

Being *justified by faith*, they enjoy *peace with God—through our Lord Jesus Christ*. This does not constitute immunity from the exigencies of life, but more resembles a wind to our back. As such, it serves as an encouragement to press ahead, in spite of obstacles and uncertainties. Since *faith* has *gained access* to God's enabling *grace*, wherein we confidently take our *stand*.

Furthermore, *we rejoice in the hope of the glory of God*. "Christians are able to take courage in present afflictions because they know that the present reality is not the final reality. This passage sets the believer's sights confidently on the future where God's glory will overcome sin and pain, where 'what is mortal may be swallowed up by life' (2 Cor. 5:4)."[4]

Then, too, suffering can reap positive results. In detail, it fosters *perseverance*. Since the latter must be invoked to manage the former. Perseverance, in turn, builds *character*. Which should be obvious. Character, moreover, solicits *hope*. Thus hope appears as a virtue.

And hope does not disappoint us. "It recalls, despite everything to the contrary, that the believer's trust in the gospel is not empty fantasy. For the Greek hope was little more than an eventuality, a possible outcome of current circumstances. But for the Jews and Christians hope is anchored to the person and promises of God."[5] As confirmed by *his love poured out into our hearts by the Holy Spirit given* to *us*.

"We know that the whole creation has been groaning as in the pains of childbirth right up to the present time," Paul allows. "Not only so, but we ourselves, who have the firstfruits of the Spirit, groan inwardly as we wait eagerly for our adoption as sons, the redemption of our bodies" (Rom. 8:22–23). He thus depicts creation

---

4. Edwards, *op. cit.*, 135–36.
5. Ibid., 137.

Hope

as suffering from man's defection, and awaiting along with him deliverance from the present bondage.

Also worthy of note, the resurrection of the body constitutes a radical departure from the classical notion of the immortality of the soul. Physicist Paul Davies writes as re-gards recent developments: "While on the one hand these studies leave little room for the traditional idea of the soul, on the other hand they leave open the possibility of survival of the personality."[6]

For in this hope we were saved," the apostle continues. "But hope that is seen is no hope at all. Who hopes for what he already has? But if we hope for what we do not yet have, we wait for it patiently." *Hope* is thus depicted as the stance of one who is saved by grace through faith. It is also a reminder that we live toward the future.

"If only for this life we have hope in Christ, we are to be pitied more than all men" (1 Cor. 15:19). *If only* implies that *hope* embraces this life, but not exclusively. There remains the life to come. As for the former, it serves as an earnest of what is yet to come. As for the latter, it provides full recompense.

Hope in Christ serves as a reminder of Paul's signature expression, explored early on. If *in Christ*, then enjoying the blessings of God. Conversely, if *in Christ*, then participating in his suffering.

This text recalls Blaise' Pascal's famous wager: "If we believe that God exists, and he does, we have everything to gain; if we believe that he does not exist, and he does, we have everything to lose; if we believe that he exists, and he does not, we have still lived the best of lives." Then in what sense is the believer to be pitied? Presumably, because having had life enriched, it proves fruitless in the end.

"For this reason, ever since I heard about your faith in the Lord Jesus and your love for all the saints, I have not stopped giving thanks for you," Paul assures his readers (Eph. 1:15–16). Having interceded on their behalf concerning the acquisition of *wisdom* and *revelation*, he adds: "I pray also that the eyes of your heart may be enlightened in order that you may know the hope to

---

6. Davies, *God and the New Physics*, 99.

which he has called you, the riches of his glorious inheritance in the saints, and his incomparably great power for us who believe."

In other words, he petitions that they be fully informed concerning the dimensions of their faith. Of prime importance is the blessed hope to which they have been called, as pertains to their *glorious inheritance*, and *incomparably great power*. In greater detail, "After the apostle has mentioned the hope of God's calling and the glory of God's inheritance, he is led to contemplate the power of God that makes all that possible. The power of God that is at work in the believer is the same power that is manifested in the resurrection, exaltation, and universal dominion of Christ."[7]

"For it is by grace you have been saved, through faith—and this not from yourselves, it is the gift of God—not by works, so that no one can boast," the apostle cautions (Eph. 2:8). "Therefore, remember that formerly you who are Gentiles by birth, (and) remember that at that time you were separate from Christ excluded from citizenship in Israel and foreigners to the covenants of the promise, without hope and without God in the world." Consequently, take full advantage of your current standing in Christ.

The desperateness of their former situation is emphasized by a series of exclusions: *from citizenship in Israel*, apart from *the covenants of promise, without hope*, and *without God in the world*. Only in the light of their subsequent redemption could they genuinely appreciate the desperate character of their prior condition.

"But now in Christ Jesus you who once were far away have been brought near through the blood of Christ" (v. 14). Whether Jew or Gentile, since all are one in Christ. As such, they were heirs of salvation and recipients of the blessed hope.

"For what is our hope, our joy, or the crown in which we will glory in the presence of our Lord Jesus when he comes?" Paul inquires. "Is it not you? Indeed, you are our glory and joy" (1 Thess. 2:19). The term for crown "commonly denoted something like a festive garland or a laurel wreath awarded to the victor at the

---

7. Patzia, *op. cit.*, 167.

games. It is likely that Paul has in mind thoughts of joyfulness and victory associated with such events."[8]

This hope is particularly associated with the role of a mentor, concerning those he has encouraged to excel. He thus anticipates the fruit of his harvest, and rejoices on behalf of those who have benefitted from his sage counsel. This is associated with their being in Christ, and faithful in their following. Accordingly, without fear of contra-diction, the best is yet to come.

8. Morris, *op. cit.*, 90.

15

Love

LOVE ROUNDS OUT THE triad of theological virtues. Its rich nuances are in some measure conveyed by the use of four Greek terms, although only the latter two play a significant role in the Biblical text. "*Storge* is the least familiar. It focuses on filial devotion. It calls attention to the love parents feel for and express toward their children, the appreciative response of their children, and the relationship between and among siblings."[1]

This recalls the saying, "Blood is thicker than water." In keeping with this notion, my brother would intercede on my behalf if I were threatened by some other youngster. He, moreover, would do so without any hesitancy.

Eros pertains to the love experienced between individuals of the opposite sex. "How beautiful you are, my darling!" the lover exclaims. "Your hair is like a flock of goats descending from Mount Gilead" (Song of Songs 4:1).

"Awake, north wind, and come south wind!" the beloved replies. "Blow on my garden, that its fragrance may spread abroad. Let my lover come into his garden and taste its choice fruits." Thus an intimate relationship is cultivated.

---

1. Inch, *Why Take the Bible Seriously?*, 63.

Philos calls attention to the shared experience of persons engaged in some common activity. In antiquity, it sometimes relates to those engaged in active academic pursuits. Conversely, we are more inclined to identify it with athletic activity. So it is that I bonded with persons in team sports.

"A friend loves at all times," the sage observes, "and a brother is born for adversity" (Prov. 17:17). As alternatively expressed, "A friend in need is a friend indeed." On the other hand, a fair-weather friend is highly suspect.

Agape is employed to characterize God's gratuitous love for those who are undeserving. In this regard, "For God so loved the world that he gave his one and only Son, that whoever believes in him shall not perish but have eternal life" (John 3:16). It was decidedly not his purpose to condemn the world, but to redeem it.

As previously allowed, this constitutes *hard love*. That is to say, because he loves us, he seeks to make us lovable. We are thus encouraged to emulate his loving compassion for others. So what if we do not feel a loving constraint for others? "Then, act toward them in a compassionate manner. It may be in the process that our feelings will catch up with our behavior. If not, let God sort out the ambiguities. He works in mysterious ways his wonders to perform."[2]

So it came to pass that Jesus inquired of Peter, "Simon, son of John, do you love me more than these?" (John 21:19). Did his devotion exceed that of the rest?

"Yes, Lord," he responded. "You know that I love you."

Whereupon, Jesus enjoined him: "Feed my lambs." Again Jesus inquired, and Peter answered in like manner. Then, when Jesus asked for a third time, the apostle protested. Jesus opts for *agape* in the first two instances, and settles for *philos* in the third, while Peter employs *philos* throughout. What are we to make of this? Perhaps nothing. Gerard Sloyan comments: "Two verbs are used in this colloquy for *love* and *feed* and two names for *sheep*. No nuance appears to be indicated, merely diversity in word use."[3]

2. Ibid, 64.
3. Sloyan, *John*, 229.

Conversely, the terms may have been deliberately selected. "If so, Peter had con-fessed confidence on the basis of a natural inclination to follow Jesus (*philos*), but this had failed him. Something more was needed, along the line of unconditional love (*agape*). In conclusion, Jesus accepts the lesser nuance, as if love in transition to some-thing more compelling."[4]

The preceding has served to prime us concerning Paul's notable discourse on love. "It is one of Paul's finest moments; indeed, let the interpreter beware lest too much analysis detract from its sheer beauty and power. Unfortunately, however, the love affair with this love chapter has also allowed it to be read regularly apart from its context, which does not make it less true but causes one to miss too much."[5] Which brings to mind the saying, "A text without its context proves to be a pretext."

In particular, the apostle has been discussing spiritual gifts. He affirms that while there are differences, these derive from the same Spirit and serve the common good. Whereas not all employ the same gifts, "eagerly desire the greater gifts. And now I will show you the most excellent way" (1 Cor. 12:31). Given the flow of his argument, it would seem that *the greater gifts* pertain to means whereby others may be edified.

"Follow the way of love," he admonishes in conclusion, "and eagerly desire spiritual gifts, especially the gift of prophecy" (14:1). Expressly in that it is set over against speaking in tongues, since the latter is unintelligible unless interpreted.

Therefore, love constitutes *the most excellent way*. "Thus it is not 'love versus gifts' that Paul has in mind, but 'love as the only context for gifts'; for without the former, the latter have no usefulness at all—but then neither does much of anything else in the Christian life."[6]

"If I speak in the tongues of men and of angels, but have not love, I am only a resounding gong or a clanging cymbal," the apostle declares. "If I have the gift of prophecy and can fathom all

---

4. Inch, *Two Gospel Motifs*, 158.
5. Fee, *The First Epistle to the Corinthians*, 625–26.
6. Ibid., 625.

Love

mysteries and all knowledge, and if I have a faith that can move mountains, and have not love, I am nothing. If I give all I possess to the poor and surrender my body to the flames, but have not love, I gain nothing" (13:1–3).

While able to entertain spiritual truths, undertake great tasks, and share generously; if lacking love, these are of little import. Irenaeus allows "but without love all are hollow and vain; moreover, that love makes man perfect and that he who loves God is perfect, both in this world and in that which is to come. For we never cease from loving God, but in proportion as we continue to contemplate Him, so much the more do we love Him."[7]

Love thus provides the impetus for spiritual growth. But only in proportion to our reflecting on God and his gracious ways. Otherwise, one's incentive lessens with the passing of time.

"Love is patient; love is kind" (v. 4). These attributes correspond to love's passive and active roles. As for the former, love helps us deal constructively with persisting problems, opposition, and personal inadequacies. In this regard, "And we urge you, brothers, warn those who are idle, encourage the timid, help the weak, be patient with everyone" (1 Thess. 5:14). Do not return wrong for wrong, "but always try to be kind to each other and to everyone else."

Always allows for no deviation, and *everyone* permits no exception. This runs counter to our natural disposition, wherein we are inclined to show kindness to those we approve of and disregard for those we dislike. Love thus strengthens our righteous resolve, while restraining our baser instincts. Needless to say, we are all works in progress when it comes to appropriating love as a pervasive virtue.

There follows seven dispositions precluded by love. *It does not envy*. It does not begrudge others their good fortune. Whether an attractive spouse, extensive possessions, or good health.

Instead, it rejoices in the desirable situations others experience. Especially as indicative of God's blessing. Hoping, praying, and working with their best interests as a constant incentive.

---

7. Irenaeus, *Against Heresies*.

It does not boast. Such as attempts to draw inordinate attention to allegedly good intentions, considerate action, or cooperative behavior. Consequently, given to exaggera-tion and display.

Conversely, one who is modest in his or her claims. Not self-depreciating, since this errs in the opposite direction. Accordingly, one who graciously accepts commendation, but is too obsessed with courting it.

It is not proud. "Some of you have become arrogant, as if I were not coming to you," Paul protests. "But I will come to you very soon, if the Lord is willing, and then I will find out not only how these arrogant people are talking, but what power they have. For the kingdom of God is not a matter of talk but of power" (1 Cor. 4:18 –20).

"Pride goes before destruction, a haughty spirit before a fall," the sage cautions. "Better to be lowly in spirit and among the oppressed than to share plunder with the proud" (Prov. 16:16–17). "The special evil of pride is that it opposes the first principle of wisdom (the fear of the Lord) and the two great commandments. The proud man is therefore at odds with himself (8:36), his neighbor (13:10) and the Lord (16:5)."[8]

It is not rude. Accordingly, it does not act in a socially unacceptable manner. If in Arab culture, one does not cross his legs so that the bottom of his shoe is facing his associates—which is viewed as an insult. So it was when one person displayed the bottom of his shoe facing his neighbor's house, as a calculated offense.

It also recalls Nigerian students sharing with me the ways in which missionaries were discourteous. For instance, failing to make available the more comfortable chairs. On the other hand, they observed: "But we always knew that they loved us." Even though given to being rude.

It is not self-seeking. "When you come together, it is not the Lord's Supper that you eat, for as you eat, each of you goes ahead without waiting for anybody else," the apostle protests. "One remains hungry, another gets drunk" (1 Cor. 11:20–21). They are thus concerned for themselves, without consideration of others.

---

8. Kidner. *Proverbs*, 120.

Such does not qualify as *the Lord's Supper*, because that which is his is common to all. Called in Christ, we are summoned to community. Not only community as an abstract concept, but as fostered by the apostles—as Christ's delegates, and thus assuming unity, purity, and universality.

It is not easily angered. It is not readily provoked. Accordingly, it is manifestly long-suffering. As such, it is inclined to give persons the benefit of the doubt, rather than assuming a worst-case scenario.

So what if a person fails to greet you warmly? Perhaps he or she is deep in thought, or distracted by some pressing concern. Otherwise, one might not be feeling well. Or failing to make eye contact, has turned his or her attention elsewhere. Consequently, one should not be inclined to anger.

It keeps no record of wrongs. For one thing, this works adversely. One becomes discontented and bitter. It is preferable to move on into an inviting future than dwell on a disheartening past.

Also pertinent, retaliation is to be discouraged. This brings to mind a time when instead of getting even with some fellow student, I would glance knowingly at him in the corridor—as if to warn him that I would even the count when he least expected it. Then one of the most noticeable results of my conversion was that I could no longer take satisfaction in this practice. Love had done its homework.

"Love does not delight in evil but rejoices with the truth" (v. 6). These resemble the two sides of a coin. If not the one, then the other.

Evil is thus depicted as the misrepresentation of truth. "Finally, brethren," Paul affectionately addresses his readers, "whatever is true, whatever is noble, whatever is right, whatever is pure, whatever is lovely, whatever is admirable—if anything is excel-lent or praiseworthy—think about such things" (Phil. 4:8). *Whatever is true* heads the list, setting the course for what follows.

"It (love) always protects, always trusts, always hopes, always perseveres" (v. 7). This summarizes all that the apostle has alleged concerning love up to the present. He does not mean that love always believes the best about everything and everyone, but that it never ceases to have hope in circumstances and persons. It is thus able to endure obstacles and opposition.

In particular, it seeks to protect all that is good and wholesome. It also fosters trust in God's ultimate triumph and current enablement. As a result, it perseveres in hope. As such, it is be preferred as *the most excellent way.*

"Love never fails" (v. 8). As for prophecies, they will cease. As for tongues, they will be silenced. As for knowledge, it will prove to be fragmentary and misleading. "For we know in part and we prophesy in part, but when perfection comes, the imperfect disappears."

In conclusion, "And now these three remain: faith, hope, and love. But the greatest of these is love" (v. 13). These three are pre-eminent. "We see this also in the fact that the three are often linked in the New Testament and early Christian literature (Rom. 5:2-5; Gal. 5:5f; Eph. 1:15-18; 4:2-5; Col. 1:4f; 1 Thess. 1:3; 5:8; Heb. 6:10-12; 10:22-24; 1 Pet. 1:3-8, 21f; cf. Barnabas 1:4; 11:8; Polycarp 3:2f.)."[9]

Faith is one of the dominant themes in Paul's correspondence. For instance, "This righteousness from God comes through faith in Jesus Christ to all who believe. There is no difference, for all have sinned and fall short of the glory of God, and are justified freely by his grace through the redemption that came by Christ Jesus" (Rom. 3:22-24).

Hope likewise makes the short list. On the other hand, "No movement has really gripped the hearts of significant numbers of people which has given them hope. In the first centuries Christianity made a habit of taking people from the depressed classes, slaves, women, outcasts, and giving them a living hope."[10]

In any case, it is fitting that the final consideration should be *love*. While it cannot be said that God exercises faith or hope, he loves and is said to epitomize love (cf. 1 John 4:8, 16). In cultural terms, "As with the father, so with his son." Thus Christians are to exercise love, characterized by its extensive attributes—as cited above. Then to persist in this fashion, under adverse circumstances, and even when faced with martyrdom—as a privileged means of participating in Christ's suffering.

---

9. Morris, *I Corinthians*, 185.
10. Ibid.,

V

Miscellaneous

16

Sage Sayings

SAGE SAYINGS PLAYED A prominent role in my early years. "A person is as good as his word," my father would confidently affirm. As the proprietor of a village store, he had to contend with persons that failed to pay what they owed. "Take a load when you go," my mother would urge. While this was derived from the practice of carrying our dirty dishes to the sink, it came to mean that we should not expect others to do for us what we were unwilling to do for ourselves.

Sage sayings have continued to play a significant role in my more mature years. This led to the publication of a collection of sage sayings some years ago, coming readily comes to mind on this occasion. They are especially apt for an age where oral expression is experiencing a qualified revival. In this regard, "The electronic age is also an age of 'secondary orality', the orality of telephones, radio, and television, which depends on writing and print for its existence."[1]

Here today; gone tomorrow. "As for man, his days are like grass, he flourishes like a flower of the field; the wind blows over it and it is gone, and its place remembers it no more" (Psa.

---

1. Ong, *Orality and Liteacy*, 3.

103:15-16). If for no other reason, one is encouraged to invest his or her time wisely.

Jesus told a story concerning a certain rich man who had a bumper crop. "He thought to himself, 'What shall I do?' I have no place to store my crops'" (Luke 12:17). "This is what I will do," he concluded. "I will tear down my barns and build bigger ones, and there I will store all my grain and my goods. And I'll say to myself, 'You have plenty of good things laid up for many years. Take life easy; eat, drink and be merry." It apparently did not occur to him that he might share his harvest with those less fortunate.

"You fool!" God reprimanded him. "This very night your life will be demanded from you. Then who will get what you have prepared for yourself?" "This is how it will be with anyone who stores up things for himself but is not rich toward God," Jesus pointedly added.

∽∽∽

This is the first day of the rest of your life. I was reminded in this connection that it did not matter how many times I fell, but how often I scrambled to my feet. It does not help to dwell on past failures, unless it is for the purpose of not repeating them.

"'Come, follow me.' Only three words, they speak a volume. He repeated them more than once: at the calling of Peter and Andrew (Matt. 4:19), in response to the disciple who requested first to bury his parents (8:22), when calling Matthew (9:9), and after admonishing a young man to sell all that he had and give to the needy (19:21)."[2] These were likely only representative instances, calling for a decisive action.

∽∽∽

Hell is filled with good intentions. Good intentions need to be activated. Otherwise, they remain dormant and inoperative.

"Show me your faith without deeds, and I will show you my faith by what I do," James proposes. "You believe that there is one God. Good! Even the demons believe that—and shudder"

---

2. Inch, *Exhortations of Jesus According to Matthew* and *Up From the Depths*, 11-12.

Sage Sayings

(2:18-19). Faith when not accompanied by appropriate action is tragically ineffectual.

❧

A tree with deep roots never fears a storm (Romanian proverb). Of similar intent, Jesus observed: "Therefore everyone who hears these words of mine and puts them into practice is like a wise man who built his house on the rock. The rain came down, the streams rose, and the winds blew and beat against that house; yet it did not fall, because it had its foundation on the rock" (Matt. 7:24-25).

"But everyone who hears these words of mine and does not put them into practice is like a foolish man who built his house on sand. The rain came down, the streams rose, and the winds blew and beat against that house, and it fell with a great crash." When he had said these things, the crowd was amazed that he taught with authority—unlike the rabbis who were careful to cite precedent.

❧

Faith can remove mountains. This is likely derived from Jesus' comment: "If you have faith as small as a mustard seed, you can say to the mountain, 'Move from here to there' and it will move" (Matt. 17:20). Thus hyperbole is calculated to greatly enhance the didactic intent.

He may have had in mind the occasion when Herod removed the top of a nearby hill to raise the elevation of the Herodium, thought to be the burial place of Herod. Jesus was a builder of a different sort, whose works have proven to be vastly superior and of con-tinuing significance. Whether in this connection or some other, a little faith in a great God is calculated to accomplish wonders.

❧

God opens the door for us to enter. This recalls a time when Paul and his com-panions "tried to enter Bithynia, but the Spirit of Jesus would not allow them to" (Acts 16:7). Whether through some overt means, or by way of perception, we are not told. The apostle subsequently had a vision of a man pleading with him, "Come over to Macedonia and help us." Concluding that God meant for them to preach the gospel in Macedonia, they prepared themselves to take their leave.

It is not always easy to recognize what constitutes a closed door. For instance, meager results at the outset may give way to more substantial gains in the future. It is not less certain what constitutes an open door, since seeming success may prove to be superficial. Consequently, one is encouraged to diligently seek divine guidance.

∞∞

God knows best. Circumstances often do not appear favorable. At such times, we may be tempted to despair. However, it is not uncommon that these are the more fortuitous occasions for spiritual growth.

"To keep me from becoming conceited because of these surpassingly great revela-tions, there was given me a thorn in the flesh," Paul reflects. "Three times I pleaded with the Lord to take it away from me. But he said to me, 'My grace is sufficient for you, for my power is made perfect in weakness.' Therefore I will boast all the more gladly about my weaknesses, so that Christ's power may rest on me" (2 Cor. 12:7–9).

His *thorn in the flesh* is variously identified. If a physical problem, perhaps poor eyesight or some lingering illness; if associated with circumstances, then likely the burden of ministering to the fledgling churches and/or persisting opposition. In any case, he experiences compensating *grace* and enabling power. As a result, he rejoices in the deficiencies that would otherwise prove to be discouraging.

∞∞

When nothing else works, read the instructions. "All Scripture is God-breathed and is useful for teaching, rebuking, correcting and training in righteousness," Paul assures his readers, "so that the man of God may be thoroughly equipped for every good work" (2 Tim. 3:16). Since it provides divine instruction on how life should be lived, to ignore its teaching is utter folly.

In greater detail, it is useful for *teaching*. This appears to be Timothy's prime responsibility in the light of the Pauline correspondence. It is also helpful for *rebuking*, which is the other side of the task. Accordingly, he is to employ Scripture to expose the errors of false teachers. It is likewise pertinent for *correcting*. While a companion of rebuking, it emphasizes ethical considerations. It is no less relevant for *training in righteousness*, which serves as the counterpart to correction. All things considered, this serves to equip *the man of God for every good work*.

He who eats or drinks and blesses not the Lord is as he that steals (Talmudic proverb). Stealing is thus portrayed as a failure to give due recognition. Jewish tradition extends this to those who demean the reputation of others. It was thought applicable in a wide range of other circumstances, such as the failure to remunerate promptly. Of course, this might work a hardship on the employee.

Thankfulness plays an important role in moral behavior. For instance, it was con-sidered an aspect of honoring one's parents. As noted previously, this had wide-ranging implications: in terms of obedience, taking care of their various needs, and appreciatively recalling them with appropriate memorials. Thus a moral legacy was enhanced from one generation to the next.

Too many cooks spoil the stew. "No man can serve two masters," Jesus cautioned. "Either he will hate the one and love the other, or he will be devoted to the one and despise the other" (Matt. 6:24). As for apt commentary, "We piously affirm that we have chosen to serve God, not mammon, but in our daily life it is mammon that sets our priorities and determines our choices. We would like to show a more bountiful eye toward the poor, but we cannot, because we need so much for ourselves."[3]

As elaborated further, "We plan to be more charitable in the future, but at the moment there are too many things we have to

---

3. Hare, *op. cit.*, 73.

buy. We work overtime or at a second job rather than spend time with our children, because there is so much that we want to get for them." This results in the previously mentioned *home alone* syndrome, as an instance of trying to serve two conflicting agendas.

⸻

Don't count your chickens before they hatch. "Now listen, you who say, 'Today or tomorrow we will go to this or that city, spend a year there, carry on business and make money.' Why, you do not even know what will happen tomorrow," James vigorously protests. "What is your life? You are a mist that appears for a little while and then vanishes" (4:13–14).

"Instead, you ought to say, 'If it is the Lord's will, we will live and do this or that.' As it is, you boast and brag. All such boasting is evil." Since it misrepresents life, and distorts priorities. "Anyone, then, who knows the good he ought to do and doesn't do it, sins." Accordingly, learn and live.

⸻

We are all Adam's children (Spanish proverb). Both as regards our divine origin and fallen estate. As for the former, all persons are worthy of consideration. Not only with regard to meeting their varied needs, but in allowing for the distinctive contribution they can make to the common good.

As for the latter, we are again reminded that "all have sinned and fall short of the glory of God" (Rom. 3:23). When coupled with the previous observation, this gave rise to the sage observation: "There is so much good in the worst of us, and so much evil in the best of us, that one should take care how he or she faults another."

In this regard, Jesus inquired: "Why do you look at the speck of sawdust in your brother's eye and pay no attention to the plank in your own eye?" (Matt. 7:3). First remove the plank from your own eye, and then you can see more clearly to remove the speck in your brother's eye. As it is, one is disposed to minimize his or her own faults, while maximizing those of others.

⸻

Sage Sayings

Should a camel get his nose in the tent, you will soon be sitting outside (Arab proverb). Jewish tradition makes extensive reference to evil inclination (*yetzer*), which must be vigorously resisted so as not to gain control. With this in mind, it urged that we build fences so not yield to temptation. While thought a legitimate practice, meticulous observance was not to suffice for divine worship.

This gave rise to the notion of the bloody nose Pharisee, who lest he lust after an attractive women, crash into a wall—causing him to bleed. He was contrasted with a .Such preserved a healthy respect for life, while raising it to a higher level.

It takes a stone to produce a pearl. "Faith fashions virtue out of adversity. We ought not to complain about that which God employs for our own good."[4] Otherwise, adversity simply compounds the problem.

"Anyone who loves his father or mother more than me is not worthy of me; anyone who loves his son or daughter more than me is not worthy of me, and anyone who does not take his cross and follow me is not worthy of me," Jesus protested. "Whoever finds his life will lose it, and whoever loses his life for my sake will find it" (Matt. 10:37–39). Such constituted the cost of discipleship, as pertains to what is lost and gained.

To whom little is not enough, nothing is enough (Greek proverb). Greed can never be satisfied. "I know what it is to be in need, and I know what it is to have plenty," Paul allowed. "I have learned the secret of being content in any and every situation" (Phil. 4:12). "What is striking, of course, is his insistence that he knows the secret of *both* plenty and want. But he did not choose 'want' as a way of life; rather he had learned to accept whatever came his way, knowing that his life was not conditioned by either, and that his relationship to Christ made one or the other essentially irrelevant."[5]

4. Inch, *Sage Sayings*, 39.
5. Fee, *Paul's Letter to the Philippians.*, 433.

Generosity plays a constructive counterpart to greed. As relates to our possessions, time, and talents. Industry in anticipation of generosity, so that we can better serve to alleviate the needs of others. Bearing in mind Jesus' appraisal, "It is more blessed to give than to receive" (Acts 20:35).

Bibliography

Anderson, Francis. *Job*. Downers Grove: Inter-Varsity, 1974.
Barnett, Paul, *The Second Epistle to the Corinthians*. Grand Rapids: Eerdmans, 1997.
Bauman, Michael. "The Dangerous Samaritan: How We Unintentionally Injure the Poor," *God and Caesar* (Bauman and Hall, eds.), 201–15
———. and David Hall (eds.). *God and Caesar*. Camp Hill: Christian Publications, 1994.
Bellinger, W. H., Jr. *Leviticus, Numbers*, Peabody: Hendrickson, 2005.
Bingham, D. Jeffrey. "Ireneaus and the Kingdom of the World," *God and Caesar* (Bauman and Hall, eds.), 27–40.
Bonhoeffer, Dietrich. *Ethics*. New York: Macmillan, 1965.
Broyles, Craig. *Psalms*. Peabody: Hendrickson, 2005.
Bruce, F. F. *The Books of Acts*. Grand Rapids: Eerdmans, 1958
———. *The Epistle to the Hebrews*. Grand Rapids: Eerdmans, 1990.
Carter, James. *John*. Nashville: Broadman, 1984.
Clement of Alexandria. *The Instructor*.
———. *The Stromata*.
Cole, R. Alan. *Exodus*. Downers Grove: Inter-Varsity, 1973.
Colson, Charles and Nancy Pearcey. *How Shall We Live?*, Wheaton: Tyndale, 1999.
Davids, Peter. *The First Epistle of Peter*. Grand Rapids: Eerdmans, 1990.
Davies, Paul. *God and the New Physics*. New York: Simon & Schuster, 1983.
Day, Gardiner. *The Apostles' Creed*. New York: Scribner's, 1963.
Dulles, Avery. *Models of the Church*. New York: Doubleday, 1987.
Eckstein, Yechiel. *How Firm a Foundation*. Brewster: Paraclete, 1997.
Edwards, John. *Romans*. Peabody: Hendrickson, 1992.
Epistle to Diognetus.
The Epistle of Polycarp to the Ephesians.
(Bauman and Hall, eds.), 7–25.
Fee, Gordon, *The First Epistle to the Corinthians*. Grand Rapids: Eerdmans, 1987.

Bibliography

———. *Paul's Letter to the Philippians*, Grand Rapids: Eerdmans, 1995.
———. *1 and 2 Timothy, Titus*. Peabody: Hendrickson, 1993.
Guthrie, Donald. *The Pastoral Epistles*. Grand Rapids: Eerdmans, 1992.
Hagner, Donald. *Hebrews*. Peabody: Hendrickson, 1993.
Hare, Douglas. *Matthew*. Louisville: John Knox, 1993.
Haring, Bernard. *The Law of Christ*, 3 vols. Westminster: Newman, 1963–1966.
Hartley, John. *Genesis*. Peabody: Hendrickson, 2003.
Hubbard, David Allan. *Joel & Amos*. Downers Grove: Inter-Varsity, 1989.
Humanist Manifesto I.
Ignatius. *To the Ephesians*.
———. *To the Romans*.
Inch, Morris. *In Christ and On Track*. Lanham: University Press of America, 2008.
———. *Devotions with David*. Lanham: University Press of America,, 2000.
———. *The Enigma of Justice*. Eugene: Wipf & Stock, 2010.
———. *Exhortations of Jesus According to Matthew* and *Up From the Depths*. Lanham: University Press of America, 1997.
———. *Pain As a Means of Grace*. Eugene: Wipf & Stock, 2009.
———. *Sage Sayings*. Edmonton: Commonwealth, 1997.
———. *Thumbs Up For the Family*. Durham: Eloquent, 2010.
———. *Two Gospel Motifs*. Lanham: University Press of America, 2001.
———. *Understanding Bible Prophecy*. New York: Harper & Row, 1977.
———. *Why Take the Church Seriously?*. Baltimore: Publish America, 2006.
Irenaeus. *Against Heresies*.
Justin Martyr. *Dialogue with Trypho*.
Kaiser, Walter, Jr. *Toward Old Testament Ethics*. Grand Rapids: Zondervan, 1983.
Kidner, Derek. *Proverbs*. Downers Grove: Inter-Varsity, 1964.
Land, Richard & Louis Moore (eds.). *Citizen Christians*. Nashville: Broadman & Holman, 1994.
Lewis, C. S. *Mere Christianity*. New York: Harper Collins, 2001.
Marshall, I. Howard. *The Epistles of John*. Grand Rapids, Eerdmans, 1978.
Mays, James. *Psalms*. Louisville: John Knox, 1994.
The Martyrdom of Ignatius.
Morris, Leon. *1 Corinthians*. Grand Rapids: Eerdmans, 1990.
———. *The First and Second Epistles to the Thessalonians*. Grand Rapids: Eerdmans, 1991.
———. *The Gospel According to John*. Grand Rapids: Eerdmans, 1995.
Mounce, Robert. *Matthew*. Peabody: Hendrickson, 1991.
Murphy, R. and E. Huwiler. *Proverbs, Ecclesiastes, Song of Songs*. Peabody: Hendrickson, 1999.
The Octavius of Minucius Felix.
Ong, Walter. *Orality & Literacy*. New York: Mathuen, 1982.
Patai, Raphael. *The Arab Mind*. New York: Scribner's, 1983.

Bibliography

———. *Society, Culture, and Change in the Middle East.* Philadelphia: University of Pennsylvania, 1971.
Patzia, Arthur. *Ephesians, Colossians, Philemon.* Peabody: Hendrickson, 1993.
Pope Paul VI. "Humane Vitae."
Robinson, George. *Essential Judaism.* New York: Pocket, 2000.
Sloyan, Gerard. *John.* Atlanta: John Knox, 1988.
Tertullian. *An Answer to the Jews.*
———. *On Modesty.*
Thielicke, Helmet. *I Believe.* Philadelphia: Fortress, 1974.
Tivnan, Edward. *The Moral Imagination.* New York: Simon & Schuster, 1995.
Wenham, Gordon. *Genesis 1–15.*
Westerhoff, John III. *Living the Faith Community.* San Francisco: Harper & Row, 1985.
Williams, David. *Acts.* Peabody, Hendrickson, 1993.
Witherington, Ben III. *The Jesus Quest: The Third Search For the Jew of Nazareth.* Downers Grove: InterVarsity, 1997.
Wright, Christopher. *Deuteronomy.* Peabody: Hendrickson, 1996.

www.ingramcontent.com/pod-product-compliance
Lightning Source LLC
Chambersburg PA
CBHW071440160426
43195CB00013B/1983